And when Jesus had cried out again in a loud voice, he gave up his spirit. At that moment the curtain of the temple was torn in two from top to bottom. The earth shook, the rocks split and the tombs broke open. The bodies of many holy people who had died were raised to life. They came out of the tombs after Jesus' resurrection and went into the holy city and appeared to many people.

—MATTHEW 27:50–53 (NIV)

MYSTERIES & WONDERS *of the* BIBLE

Unveiled: Tamar's Story
A Life Renewed: Shoshan's Story

MYSTERIES & WONDERS of the BIBLE

A LIFE RENEWED

SHOSHAN'S STORY

Ginger Garrett

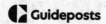 Guideposts

A Gift from Guideposts

Thank you for your purchase! We want to express our gratitude for
your support with a special gift just for you.

Dive into **Spirit Lifters**, a complimentary e-book
that will fortify your faith, offering solace during
challenging moments. Its 31 carefully selected
scripture verses will soothe and uplift your soul.

Please use the QR code or go to **guideposts.org/
spiritlifters** to download.

Mysteries & Wonders of the Bible is a trademark of Guideposts.

Published by Guideposts
100 Reserve Road, Suite E200, Danbury, CT 06810
Guideposts.org

This is a work of fiction. While the characters and settings are drawn from
scripture references and historical accounts, apart from the actual people, events,
and locales that figure into the fiction narrative, all other names, characters, places,
and events are the creation of the author's imagination or are used fictitiously.
Every attempt has been made to credit the sources of copyrighted material used
in this book. If any such acknowledgment has been inadvertently omitted or
miscredited, receipt of such information would be appreciated.

Scripture references are from the following sources: *The Holy Bible, King James
Version* (KJV). *The Holy Bible, New International Version* (NIV). Copyright © 1973,
1978, 1984, 2011 by Biblica, Inc. Used by permission of Zondervan. All rights
reserved worldwide. www.zondervan.com.

Cover and interior design by Müllerhaus
Cover illustration by Brian Call represented by Illustration Online LLC.
Typeset by Aptara, Inc.

ISBN 978-1-961251-09-0 (hardcover)
ISBN 978-1-961251-54-0 (softcover)
ISBN 978-1-961251-53-3 (epub)

Printed and bound in the United States of America
10 9 8 7 6 5 4 3 2 1

A LIFE RENEWED

SHOSHAN'S STORY

GLOSSARY OF TERMS

codex • Before the Roman Empire, books were written on long scrolls. However, the invention of the codex, which is simply pages bound together, changed how we created, carried, and distributed books. The invention of the codex made copying and distributing the Bible much easier. The plural is *codices*.

denarius • an ancient Roman coin, which is mentioned several times in the New Testament. Like the modern dollar, its value fluctuated. It is estimated that one denarius was the equivalent of a day's labor at minimum wage. The plural is *denarii*.

koom • Most often used as a verb, it means to rise, to stand up, and sometimes can refer to someone who is preparing to fight.

paradise • The use of "heaven" and "paradise" in the New Testament can seem to be interchangeable, but the word *paradise* has distinct qualities that might help us understand the concept of heaven. *Paradise* in the modern Western concept means a place of bliss and perfection. The modern definition lacks any relationship to Jesus and to the story of Eden. To anyone who lived during the New Testament era, however, *paradise* called to mind something very different...

a garden. Specifically the Garden of Eden, a garden in the presence of God. When Jesus promised the thief on the cross, "Today, you will be with Me in paradise," He was assuring the dying man that a perfected, divine place awaited, a thriving, energetic new life in the presence of God.

Roman Plague • an ancient name for malaria. Lacking an understanding of viruses and bacteria and how diseases were transmitted, the ancients knew of malaria but lacked effective medical treatment. The disease, transmitted by the bite of an infected mosquito, causes fevers that come and go, fatigue, lack of appetite, and general wasting away of its victims. Despite common ancient fears, malaria was not transmittable from one victim to the next, not in the same way a common cold might be transmitted, for example. The disease was believed to be caused by "bad air," and Romans feared areas that had stagnant odors. Only one plant was known to be helpful against the Roman Plague, and few knew of it or how to use it. Malaria was especially cruel to expectant mothers, often causing the death of the child as well as the mother.

Hebrew Months of the Calendar Year versus Roman Months

The Hebrew calendar is based on cycles of both the sun and moon and corresponds to Jewish holidays. While there are no named days of the week, there is a Sabbath built into each one-week cycle. The new day begins at sundown.

The Roman calendar (or its modern equivalent, called the Gregorian calendar) is based on solar cycles. It does not rely on lunar cycles to establish dates. Each new day begins at midnight.

Here is a general chart to help understand how the calendars relate to each other.

(Hebrew month • approximate Gregorian equivalent)

Shevat • January to February

Adar • February to March

Nisan • March to April

Iyar • April to May

Sivan • May to June

Tammuz • June to July

Av • July to August

Elul • August to September

Tishri • September to October

Heshvan • October to November

Kislev • November to December

Tevet • December to January

CHAPTER ONE

From her deep sleep, Shoshan heard Him.

"Shoshan, wake up." At the sound of His voice, so rich and familiar, she tried to stir and open her eyes, but something pinned her arms to her sides. Besides, her eyelids were so heavy.

"The veil is torn," He whispered. "But wait for Me."

His palm rested lightly over the hollow of her throat. Warmth from His hand flooded over her cool skin. She sensed that He leaned down, His face inches from hers as He breathed the words of life. His breath was a soft breeze, like the first spring morning after a bitter winter.

She inhaled, a gasping sound, as His breath entered her body, sweeping away darkness, loosening stiff muscles. She struggled to open her eyes. She only wanted to say His name and look into His eyes again.

The bindings on her sides held fast. Shoshan fought against them, and suddenly she was alone in the darkness. She sensed that He was not here with her anymore. He had gone somewhere, a deeper place, a more dreadful darkness. How she knew this, she could not say. He had left her here, but not forever. He would return.

She felt life returning to her limbs. Her chest rose and fell as breath moved in her body. It was good to lie here in the grave and wait.

Sometime later, Shoshan awoke. How long she had dozed peacefully in the darkness, she did not know. When she still couldn't open her eyes, she realized her face was swathed in linen. There was a light near her feet. She could see the glow through the bindings around her head. Her body rested on a flat hard rock, as if she had merely stretched out for a nap. The rock was uncomfortable, digging into her shoulder blades and hips. She wanted to stand up and rub her arms for warmth. Had the world always been this cold? She could not remember.

She inhaled deeply again, but this time a strip of fabric was sucked into her mouth. Spitting it out, she wiggled her head side to side then up and down to loosen the bindings. When the lower half of her face was free, she breathed in big, greedy inhalations, ignoring the brackish smell around her. There was another scent too, a strong woodsy note, like… myrrh. Yes, it was myrrh. Myrrh and cassia, too, were heavy in the air, but just underneath was the sickening sweetness of rot.

Unnerved by that rotting scent, she worked to free her right hand. With that done, she tore at the linen strips around her face and body. They had been soaked in oil and easily tore away in her hand. She struggled to remember what she was doing or where she had just been. Had she woken from a dream, or was she in a dream? The light near her feet beckoned her.

She was in a cold, dark cave, one where the dead were buried. But she was alive. Who had bandaged her like this and why? Had she been injured? Slowly, her mind pieced together little bits of memory, like mending tears in a garment, bringing jagged edges together, trying to make them fit.

Jesus had been here. Something in the cave was different, in a way that could only be explained by His presence. He shifted the atmosphere in a way that no one could explain.

And she remembered that now, how His presence changed a room. She had been with Him before, before waking like this, back when He taught people in the hills and blessed a boy's fish and bread. It had mesmerized her, how He had blessed the meager portion before breaking it, and after He broke it, He gave it away. Somehow, that moment stayed with her above all the others. Blessed, broken, given. After that, those three words became a chant under her breath, the rhythm for her days.

Even when…

Her mind snapped shut, not wanting to show her its secrets. Not yet, not until she was free and standing in the sun.

The light at her feet told her there was an entrance not far, although it was partially covered by a stone or a door. If she could free her legs, she could get out. Something told her she had to, that He was ready for her to walk out.

She wiggled and pushed her body until both arms were free. Ripping the remaining linens off her legs, she stood next to a wall in the shadows, panting from exertion. Something furry and warm scampered across her foot, and she shrieked, jumping back, one hand out to brace herself in case she stumbled. Her hand pressed against the wall, dislodging a pile of old dry bones. The bones rained down, covering her feet and calves.

She stared at the bones on the ground as her knees began to tremble. And the myrrh was so strong, yet she never used it as a body oil or in her wash. Lifting a strip of linen from her shoulder to her nose, she inhaled again the sharp, spicy scent. Myrrh was used for the dead.

Now she knew she was right. She was standing in a grave, surrounded by the dead. *But no,* Shoshan corrected herself, *I am standing in my grave. Someone put me here, like I was dead.*

I was dead.

An involuntary shudder ran through her.

The stone that stood at the entrance of the cave had a huge crack running through its center. Edging toward it, feeling her legs move as they once did, marveling at the sensation of the cold dirt under her feet, she pressed her palms flat against the stone, inhaling sharply. It was cold and smooth to the touch. She ran her palms over it, feeling the surface, her arms tingling as if each sensation was a marvelous discovery.

She felt weightless, like she could walk through the break in the stone if she wanted, walk right out.

Had she been dead? The thought was strange. That was impossible. She wasn't a ghost, was she? Every child in Rome was raised on mythical stories about ghosts and monsters. Those stories popped up in her mind, as if that was the explanation. Pressing harder against the stone, she felt her muscles flexing. She had always been told that ghosts had no physical body. But she had a body, so clearly she was more than a spirit.

From the other side, she could hear voices. An argument had broken out. The harsh tones made her step back, away from the light. She had forgotten how anger sounded, how it made her heart speed up. But if one of them had peered into the grave, through the stone, maybe they were arguing out of fright. Neither knew what hid in the darkness.

"It is all right! I am alive!" she shouted. The voices went abruptly silent.

"Can you hear me?" she called again, louder. No reply came. Someone had been on the other side, though, just a moment before. Someone must have heard her.

The stone groaned as it was pushed to one side. Someone pushed it for her. She would thank them. Eagerly, she stepped through the gap into the open air. The light pierced her eyes, and she threw her arm over her face, her eyes watering. After blinking back the tears, she slowly lowered her arm and looked. She was alone.

She was on a hillside, just above a lovely city made from limestone bricks that glittered in the sun. Below, fruit trees had emerald green leaves with waving white blossoms.

Sitting down beside the stone, she breathed deeply. The air was fresh and she drank it in, feeling the wind whoosh in and out of her lungs, a delicious sensation. She could spend the whole day just sitting here breathing the cool garden air. Below her, the grass was brilliant green. The sun on her shoulders was tender.

Life was a miracle. But maybe this was all a dream? Surveying the city below, recognition hit her with a jolt.

Jerusalem! Oh, I remember you!

It was spring, and she was in Jerusalem. She lived here, didn't she? Yes, she remembered that much now. She lived here with her husband Antonius and her... Her hand fluttered over her abdomen. Her mind snapped shut again.

Do not panic. Think. Where am I?

She was on the north end of Jerusalem, on the other side of the hill where criminals were executed. The thought made her cold. Concentrating, she closed her eyes and inhaled again. It was there, yes, a faint but sharp odor of old blood. Someone had been crucified there recently, maybe days ago. She had to get home to her husband, Antonius. She had been raised to life, but everything else remained shrouded in her memory. He would remember though. Antonius was a shrewd man.

Down to her far right, the temple was visible, and directly beneath her was the city wall. Everywhere around her were tombs. Some were sealed, as they had been for generations. Others, like hers, stood open, the stones rolled away. Many stones were cracked as if by violent force. The cracks split the rocks wide enough to illuminate the graves within. The graves were empty, and linen strips littered the garden path.

She needed to follow that path down the garden's hill, back into the city of Jerusalem. Someone had been just outside the grave, arguing. She had heard them. Something was terribly wrong, but she did not know what it was.

Putting her hands on the ground to stand, she caught sight of her left hand. Her marriage band, a solid gold ring with a square ruby, was missing. She never took it off. Never. It was a symbol of her husband's devotion, which had waned of late. She remembered that with a groan. The band was a constant comfort, and she had polished it every afternoon before napping. She had been so tired since... Since...

Two young men dashed out from behind a stone below her on the path.

"Wait!" she called.

They did not look back but ran as if terrified. They had been the ones she'd heard fighting, she was sure of it. But what was scaring them? She was only a woman, unarmed and alone. They were young men in their prime. Looking around, she saw nothing that could intimidate them. Unless... Had her appearance changed terribly? She touched her face and examined her hands and arms, but she did not see or feel any deformities.

Then the events of her last day came rushing back. Pressing a hand to her forehead, as if she could stop them from crashing through her mind, she whimpered as each memory surfaced, one after the other. The young men were scared of her because her beating heart defied natural law. No one walked out of the grave.

She remembered that she had been in a bed, her head hurting so badly it was as if the pain were a bolt of lightning. She had heard the voices of her husband and another woman she did not know. The woman was... The name was just out of reach. Shoshan did not know her, and was not friends with her, she was sure of that. Why had a stranger been in her bedchamber?

And she was sure there was something more. She had been in bed at that last moment of her life, but just before that, she remembered crouching on all fours, like an animal, panting and groaning. The thought horrified her. What had happened?

She had to get home. Everything felt wrong, and she sensed danger in the air. If the Romans were in a crucifying mood, she did not want to be alone on the streets. Only too recently, the Romans had crucified two thousand men at once for revolting against taxes. The terror, the smell and sounds... She had been afraid to leave her home for days afterward.

A woman hurrying over the hill saw her standing there and gasped in fright. Two men following behind shook their fists at Shoshan.

"They will find the body!" one of them yelled. "And the lot of you will be crucified for this! Jesus was just the beginning!"

Shoshan froze, her breath caught in her chest. How exactly did those men know she had been dead and come back to life? Had they seen her in the cemetery?

One of the men leered at her before he hurried away, and she realized she was dressed only in a thin linen tunic, nothing more than a sleeping gown. Instinctively, her hand went to her hair. There was no veil covering her head.

She wore immodest bedclothes and had no veil to signify she was a married woman. Never would she dream of walking in public like this.

Grabbing a discarded length of linen from the ground, she wrapped it around her shoulders and then grabbed another, wider strip, trying to create a makeshift robe. More people came over the hill now, dazed and pale, as if in shock. Shoshan saw the scene as they did, a garden filled with broken graves. She watched as people looked inside the graves and shrieked in fright, then saw Shoshan and shrieked again.

Shoshan began to flee down the path, shocked to find her legs were strong and steady. Shouldn't her body be weaker? Her mind seized upon any evidence to refute the conclusion she had reached in the cave. Her resurrection was real. But that was hard to accept, even after experiencing it herself. Besides, she hadn't felt this good since…

What was it that nagged at her? So much of her memory was still gone.

There was no time to stop and think. Everywhere, she saw open graves, sealing stones lying on their sides, burial linens piled just outside the entrances. All around her, people were shouting. Some of the younger ones raced ahead of her, their eyes wild with fear or hope.

Shoshan now had only one thought: Antonius. She had to get home to her husband. He would know what had happened. And he would know what to do next.

CHAPTER TWO

Staying close to the wall, Shoshan approached the north side of the city. The people running from the garden had dispersed back into the pilgrims and merchants entering Jerusalem. Scanning the crowds, she tried to spot anyone else wearing grave clothes. Other tombs had stood open. Where were those people? Wrapping her arms tightly around her chest, she shivered in the afternoon sun. The oil that had been rubbed onto her arms in the grave stung her nose. A few women cast sideways glances at her then grimaced at the sight of her, so poorly dressed and unveiled. None offered to help. Shoshan felt colder under their gaze. She just wanted to get home.

As she approached the Fish Gate, the smell hit her. Although her mother was a Jew, Shoshan had been raised in Rome, where there were no fresh fish markets. Everything there was imported, salted and dried. The market here sold fish from the Mediterranean and Lake Galilee. The fish sat all day in the sun. They did not smell fresh by this time of day.

Then she noticed the noise, which was as overwhelming as the smell.

"Come and buy!"

"Over here!"

"Just for you!"

As she pressed through the gate, mingling with the crowd, several fishermen stopped, their mouths open midsentence, staring at her lack of clothing. It took a lot to shock a fisherman, she knew. She could feel warmth surging to her face with the embarrassment of a strange man staring at her body through the thin material of the grave linen.

A rough-looking elderly man, his face as craggy as the hills behind them, waved a shaking hand at her, beckoning her over. On the table in front of him was a display of fresh fish.

Something about him seemed familiar. Hesitating, she relented and approached him. Why did she know his face?

While she was still searching her memory, he removed his robe and handed it to her.

"Oh, I could not, sir," she protested, even as she quickly draped it across her shoulders and pushed her arms through. She would do anything to stop the stares, even borrow a man's robe that was threadbare and had dried fish scales stuck to it along the arms.

Out of the corner of her eye, she caught a group of young fishermen counting their *denarii* and eyeing her. They thought she was a prostitute!

Quickly wrapping the tunic more tightly around her, she thanked the stranger for his robe. When her hand passed over her abdomen, a shock jolted her. She needed to remember something, something her body wanted her to know.

The man dug through the satchels at his feet. She watched, wondering what he was looking for.

Not speaking, he frowned in concentration until his hand grasped a coin. Straightening up, his face was pinched, like he was afraid too.

Why was everyone so afraid?

"Take this to Servia at the gate. She will sell you a veil."

She studied his face a moment longer, and then the memory came to her. "Oh! I do know you! I know your sons, Simon and Andrew."

His eyes cleared immediately, and he glared at her, lifting one finger to his lips to silence her. Leaning across the table, he motioned for her to lean toward him.

"Have you seen them today?" he whispered.

"No," she admitted. "Were they in the cemetery too?"

"God forbid!" he gasped, jerking backward.

She raised her eyebrows and shook her head. "Did I offend you? I did not mean to. I just… I saw people running away from the cemetery. I thought you meant they had been there too."

His glare softened, just barely. He moved closer, and his voice became soft. "If you walked with Jesus, get off the streets as fast as you can."

He turned away from her, shouting out for customers, ignoring her. He would not look at her again.

Shoshan felt as if every eye was upon her, and she did not know why. She had a robe on now, at least. But still, people stared. What was happening? Hurrying to buy a veil, Shoshan exhaled in relief as she whipped the thin fabric over her head and face. Now nothing would bring attention to her. She looked like any other respectable wife, out for the day's shopping.

Leaving the Fish Gate market, she hurried along the street toward the living district, where her modest home was. The very thought made her feet move more quickly. She would be home, and shut the door, and be in Antonius's arms in just a few more minutes.

All along the street, people stopped and slowly turned, staring at her before she even passed by. When they saw her, their eyes ran up and down, as if they were perplexed. Then their expressions turned to astonishment or terror. Mothers grabbed their children's hands and yanked them close. Men scowled, and their hands turned to fists, or else they crossed their arms, glaring at her. What was her crime? How was she offending them? She reached up to touch her face once more, then looked at her fingers. They were pink and full, with no grime on them. Her face was clean. But something was scaring people, that was obvious.

Walking even more quickly, she passed a shop that sold mirrors and women's clothes, with the door propped open to encourage a breeze. She went inside to look at herself in the mirror. Studying her reflection, she could see no physical change, although her countenance had an otherworldly glow. Or was that just a trick of the light? Touching her face, she was relieved to find it warm and soft, the familiar face of a woman in her midtwenties, a bloom of health in her cheeks, her brown eyes bright and wide. Her hair cascaded down her shoulders, neatly combed and oiled.

What was so frightening about her? Maybe the strange combination of a radiant face with a grave tunic and the smell of myrrh unnerved people. Maybe something had happened in the city while she had been… She couldn't think of the appropriate word. *Dead? Sleeping?* She had no vocabulary for a temporary death.

The shopkeeper came from the back of the store and stopped. His nose wrinkled at something in the air. He was a tall man with a terribly curved spine, so that one shoulder sat much higher than the other. Shoshan's heart immediately went out to him. It looked like a painful malady to live with. Lifting a hand, she wanted to introduce herself, thinking she might come back and buy a mirror here. He needed the money for doctors, she was sure.

"By Jove!" Staring at her, he clutched the amulet on his chest. He was a Roman, then. Romans worshiped Jupiter, or Jove as he was also called, as the supreme god.

"I just wanted to—" Shoshan began.

"Get out before I call the guards!" the shopkeeper yelled.

People had gone mad. Was there poison in the water?

The shopkeeper lurched out of the store behind her.

"She is one of them!" he yelled, standing outside the shop, pointing back in at her. "She stinks of the grave!"

She pushed past him, exiting the shop. People parted from her, repelled away. Shoshan's mind whirled. She knew the myrrh had a strong fragrance, but how did these people know she was...What was she? She didn't even know!

A woman pointed to Shoshan and screamed in Aramaic. "*Koom!*"

One who stands up again, a resurrected one. But it also could mean one who intends to fight.

Shoshan threw up her hands in protest. "I just want to go home!"

A Roman guard turned the corner. His eyes locked on hers. The man was around her age, with light brown hair and brilliant green eyes. Handsome, except for a scar that ran across his left cheek and down through his jaw, from a sword, perhaps. The scar was raised and red, and it was hard not to stare at it. It must have happened when he was very young, and it must have hurt very badly. But she tore her gaze away from it as his hand raised to his sword. His breastplate caught the glare of the sun and blinded her, and she lifted her arm to shield her eyes.

"I do not want to fight," she called. Whatever rebellion was happening in these streets, she had no part in it. "I am on my way home!"

"Koom!" the woman yelled to the guard, still pointing at Shoshan.

The guard scowled and moved toward her, his hand still on his sword. Rome executed people for insurrection, she knew. The cries of "Koom!" did not stop, and the ground seemed to shake with every step the guard took toward her. Shoshan turned and ran with a speed that surprised her, shoving people aside, cutting around corners, taking stairs to streets that led to shops, and then cutting through the shops to new streets. People cursed her for knocking them down or out of the way, and no matter how fast she ran or which turns she took, she heard the calls. *Koom!* She heard the stomp of Roman boots, the clang of armor as more guards joined the first in pursuit of her.

Turning a corner, she dashed into a darkened shop that sold Roman codices. In the darkness, she fought to catch her breath. Each shuddering gasp sounded so loud in her ears, and she clenched her jaw, willing herself to be quiet.

Would the guards think to look for a Jewish girl in a Roman shop? Hopefully not. The tread of boots drew closer.

In the darkness, a hand reached for her, landing on her arm. Before she could scream, another hand clasped over her mouth, and she was pulled backward into the shadows. She struggled to break the man's hold on her, but he was stronger.

When she was released, she was in a tiny room filled with about ten other people, all strangers to her. They sat around a table, hands folded in their laps, or eating flatbreads. They looked up at her with interest, then looked at her captor as if he would explain.

No one here was afraid of her. Curious about her, yes, but not afraid. Slowly, she felt her muscles loosen, and she was able to breathe.

An oil lamp burned in the dark room, and flickering light cast dancing shadows on the walls, distorting the faces that huddled around it. Their faces seemed kind, though, as they squinted to look at her. Had it been even an hour since she stumbled out of her grave? So much had already happened. All she wanted was to go home, to see Antonius, to think that this was all a dream.

"Who are you?" she demanded, looking around the room.

The man who had grabbed and released her looked around at the others, his white bushy eyebrows jumping up and down as he chuckled.

"You are just in time," he replied, then patted her lightly on her shoulder. "We were just about to make our introductions."

Was he crazy?

A woman who seemed familiar somehow to Shoshan, though Shoshan was sure she had never seen her before, shook her head.

"You owe her more of an explanation," she scolded the man. "Poor girl is scared." She peered across the jumping flame at Shoshan. "This man has been watching for us on the street, collecting us, one by one, pulling us to safety."

"It was smart thinking to hide in this shop." The shopkeeper smiled. "There are more guards on the streets every minute."

Shoshan stared at her, then at the shopkeeper, not understanding. She had only chosen this shop because it sold Roman codices. No one staging a rebellion against Rome would be shopping for those.

"Did you wake up in a grave?" the woman pressed.

Shoshan swallowed, the noise audible in the tiny room. How did this woman guess that?

"Do not worry," the woman replied. "We all did."

"I did not wake up in a grave," an elderly man said. "I woke up in a vegetable patch. A rabbit was tugging on a radish when up I popped. I do not think the poor thing will ever eat radishes again." He grunted, suddenly dismayed. "My grave was not tended to. Someone sold it for a garden. Such a thing should not be done."

"Let us all think," the woman said. "How long have you been dead? Does anyone know?"

No one spoke.

The woman tried again. "What is the last thing you remember?"

"David was dancing through the streets." The elderly man spoke first, his face transformed by the memory. "The ark had come to Jerusalem. What joy! We feasted and sang until dawn. I was eighty years old. Glory to God."

His face cleared suddenly. "Where is the ark now? Did David finish the temple he planned for it?"

"The ark is not here," Shoshan murmured. Her mind was doing the math, trying to comprehend his statement. "And Solomon, David's son, is the one who built the temple. David was dead by then."

The man clicked his teeth. "I knew that, somehow. How did I know that?" His gaze fell to the floor, away to his right, as if searching his memories.

"Wait," one woman across from Shoshan interrupted. "I remember that I was bringing bread to the workers at the wall. King David had been gone for...Well, you are right, he was dead. Had been for generations. Jerusalem had fallen. But we had no temple, no king."

Everyone fell silent, staring into the flickering light. Jerusalem without a temple? Without a king? No wall to protect it?

"The wall still stands," Shoshan said quickly, mentally going back through the stories she knew. "And the temple was rebuilt. Nehemiah led your people, yes?"

The woman nodded vigorously. "And a king?" she asked. "Who is the king?"

"There is a man called the King of the Jews. His name is Jesus." Shoshan took a deep breath. "He is the Messiah."

"Yes," everyone murmured, a sound of joy, like water in a fast-moving brook. It was as if Shoshan was reminding them of a name that had been on the tips of their tongues, just out of reach. But how could they know of Jesus? They had been dead when He was born!

Not Shoshan though. She had spent many afternoons following Him, listening to Him teach. Antonius was not interested in the new teacher roaming the countryside, especially because the teacher was a carpenter and construction worker like Antonius. They had probably worked on the same building projects together. Still, Antonius had never stopped her from leaving to hear Jesus, not even when she was...

Her hand flew to her abdomen. *Not even when I was pregnant and close to delivery.*

Leaping to her feet, she lurched toward the door, but the older woman jumped up and caught her by the arms. Shoshan struggled and raised her voice until the shopkeeper placed his hand over her mouth again. Everyone looked stricken with fear now, their faces distorted, and she guessed they had been hunted too. She nodded, indicating that she would not scream, and he released her.

"I was pregnant," she gasped in the tiny room, trying to catch her breath as the memories crashed in. "I was in labor, and the midwife was yelling for someone, or something. That is the last thing I remember."

A different kind of silence fell over the room. No one would meet her eye. They guessed something she did not. She could see that in their eyes.

"What happened to your child?" the woman who brought bread to Nehemiah's workers asked.

Shoshan closed her eyes, thinking. "I do have one memory."

Opening her eyes, she looked around at their faces. They were all so beautiful, the joy radiating from them as if they carried a bit of heaven. Fear had looked so unnatural on them.

"I held her in my arms, and she laughed. Oh, she has dark lashes, so very long! And such delicate fingers. I think she might become an artist or a weaver. When she laughed, her eyes danced."

Shoshan shook her head. "I was so happy that I thought my heart might burst, that I had no more room to contain so much joy. I have never felt anything like it."

The women in the room exchanged glances again, then smiled at Shoshan.

"What is it?" Shoshan demanded.

The oldest woman spoke, her voice soft. "Newborns do not laugh. They cannot."

"I heard her laugh. I saw it," Shoshan responded, indignant.

"I know! I am not doubting you," the woman replied. "But it could not have happened. Not on earth."

Shoshan heard the shopkeeper clear his throat.

All her strength left her, and she slumped down, her hands pressing into her abdomen. Her memory was real, but it was a memory of another place. Jesus spoke of a place called paradise. Others called it heaven. She had been there with her daughter, hadn't she? The shattered pieces of her memory came together at once, the story making sense now.

"I died in childbirth," Shoshan said quietly. "I think my child did too." The women gathered around her, pushing the men aside, putting their arms and hands on her to comfort her. But Shoshan was confused more than stricken. She had seen her daughter, and her daughter was very much alive.

But had she seen a little body in the grave when she awoke? Shoshan tried to remember but couldn't remember anything past the little bedroom where she had been in labor. Antonius had been there, she remembered that, but did he know she was dying? Did he have a chance to say goodbye?

He must have been devastated. Utterly heartbroken. He lost his wife and daughter in the same day.

She knew that she must return home at once. Antonius needed to see her and to understand that miracles were happening.

He needed to know that anything was possible.

CHAPTER THREE

The group sat quietly, each with their own thoughts, as the oil lamp flickered and swayed. When darkness fell, they would disperse. Until then, it was not safe to leave the shop.

"Why are the Romans chasing us?" a shy young man asked, his face glowing in the lamplight. He caught Shoshan studying his face, and she looked away, embarrassed. Even if she doubted their stories, even if she doubted herself, she could not deny one fact. These ordinary people were radiant with an otherworldly beauty. Heaven was an actual place, and it had marked them, each of them, with a distinct beauty.

"They think the disciples of Jesus, His followers, have staged an elaborate prank," the shopkeeper explained. "They assume you are agitating among the people, convincing them that the dead have risen. A plot of revenge to cause civil unrest after they crucified Jesus for breaking Jewish law."

Jesus was crucified? Shoshan gasped, but she knew this too somehow. Looking at their faces stricken with sorrow, it seemed everyone did. She remembered the sound of weeping in the heavens, and a tremendous roar when sunlight burst through the darkness.

"Yes, three days ago, Jesus was crucified," the shopkeeper told her. "I watched from a great distance. The guards were so cruel, and many

Jewish people were terrified that the wrath of Rome would not be content to crucify only Jesus. The skies were dark, and a great earthquake hit the city. Graves split open. Early this morning, people came walking out. People have been spotted on the road leading into Jerusalem, people long dead, walking toward the gates, beaming with joy."

"Wait. Jesus is dead?" Shoshan murmured. Was it like her daughter, a death here on earth but alive somewhere else? She could not fathom a world without Jesus.

"He was," the shopkeeper said. "But this morning…"

The room seemed to fill with light as everyone looked at each other, grasping the situation. Jesus had returned. He had been the first to walk out of the grave. Somehow, she knew that. She had felt Him near, heard Him somehow telling her to come out.

"Jesus is alive," the young man announced, but everyone merely nodded in confirmation. Everyone knew it without being told. This resurrection was without explanation in so many ways. None of the people in the room seemed to have a plan for what to do next.

The shopkeeper pushed the heels of his palms against his eyes and then cleared his throat. His eyes were moist with tears, and Shoshan wondered why. Had he lost someone, and this talk of heaven was bittersweet?

"The people of Jerusalem are still terrified," the shopkeeper continued. "They do not know if the followers of Jesus are now trying to incite fear, or if there will be revenge for the crucifixion. And if there is revenge, we all know what Rome will do."

Rome would crush Jerusalem.

He rubbed his hands together, eager to change the subject. "You are the second group this morning that I have gotten off the streets. The

Romans must not find you, or they will arrest you. You might not know anything about a plot or be guilty of agitating in the streets, but that will not matter to them. Wait until dark and make your way home."

"Do our families know?" Shoshan asked. Did Antonius know she was alive? He must be heartbroken, and his grief still raw. It felt as though she had only been gone a short while, but she had no clear evidence of the exact length of time.

The shopkeeper bit his lip thoughtfully. "Some of the believers, a group of women, I think, the same group who witnessed Jesus's execution, saw Him after He was resurrected. They know He is alive, and I suspect they may know about you all too. As word began to spread about the resurrections, a great many citizens rushed to the cemetery, hoping their relatives were the ones brought back to life. Those who believed the stories, that is. It has been complete chaos since dawn broke this morning."

It all sounded so far-fetched that she could not blame people for their disbelief. Especially if they had never walked with or followed Jesus. How would they have been prepared for anything like this?

"But what about Jesus?" she asked the little group of refugees from the grave. "He has been resurrected, but where is He?"

Everyone glanced at each other.

"Are we supposed to do something?" she asked, more to herself. "In response to His crucifixion? Defy Rome or the Jewish priests somehow? I do not think so, but I have no idea."

"I think it is the opposite," the young man said, lifting one shoulder lightly. "We are His response to death."

"Our resurrection is a defiance of the grave," the old woman repeated softly, thinking. "I like that."

"But death is not our only enemy," the young man pointed out. "We have been hunted before. I think we had better be prepared for anything. We have no idea what Jesus is planning."

"Wait. When was Jesus crucified?" Shoshan asked suddenly. Somehow, she knew of the event, but the exact date held a clue to her own death and resurrection. If she knew the date, it would answer one question. Even so, she could ask a thousand questions and still not understand why the Lord had raised her. Or anyone in this room, especially since He had not given them a specific assignment.

"The day before the Passover Sabbath," the shopkeeper answered. "And He was raised this morning, three days after His death."

She counted in her head. When she was in labor, Jesus was with the disciples outside the city. Passover was approaching, just days away. There were rumors of death threats, and fear that the Jewish leaders would arrest Him if He entered the city for Passover, but her memory stopped there. If she died just before He did, that meant she had been dead for eight days.

"And the resurrected? We all came out at the same time?" she asked, looking around the room. "There is no chance...that someone might be left behind, still in the grave, waiting?"

"The witnesses are saying that everyone came out the same day Jesus did," the woman replied gently. "Even people coming into the city from graves in the countryside. But only adults. We have seen no children."

Her heart fell. Why wouldn't Jesus raise her newborn daughter? If all these wondrous things were happening, why not do that too?

The elderly man spoke. "People who had been dead for entire generations were resurrected, others like you, only dead a few days.

Nothing will make sense, not until Jesus explains it. But as I listen to you all, I know this: no one is sure what they are to do now, except go out and live."

"Live and speak," replied someone in the back of the room. Several nodded.

"Yes, tell of what we know."

What did they know, especially those who had been dead for years? Where would they go tonight if they had no homes anymore?

She had to concentrate on her own situation. The rest was too overwhelming. Somehow, when the sun set, she had to evade capture and get home. She had never been targeted by the Roman guards, and the thought terrified her. Their armor blinded you in the streets, the bloodred plumes of their helmets towering far above all men, the sound of their boots making dust rise in their wake. And sometimes they carried more than swords or daggers. The commanders had whips, the leather darkened by the blood of men's backs.

She stood and went to the entrance of the room. Peeking outside into the streets, she saw Jerusalem in uproar. Everywhere, the crowds clamored for safety from the dead they said were walking, while some sat blocking the street, weeping with joy. She guessed the ones who felt so much joy were Jesus followers, knowing that miracles abounded in the city today. Roman soldiers stood at the head of the street, faces flushed and angry. Stones littered the ground, and buildings had gaping holes, like missing teeth, where the rocks had fallen in the earthquake.

A Sadducee priest stood in the very spot where Shoshan had been seen, the jewels in his robe's clasp catching the last of the late afternoon light. Fear shot through her body. A Sadducee? Why would a priest, especially a Sadducee, be involved in this? The hairs along the back of her neck rose. The Sadducees had hated Jesus. Sadducees did not believe in the afterlife, the possibility of resurrection, or any revelation of God that was not recorded in the Torah. For them, the written law was everything. Nothing else—no one else—mattered. Sadducees would be especially furious over the resurrections, even if they believed they were only rumors.

She looked at her hands, finding a speck of dirt from the grave and wiping it away. Days ago, she'd been dead. The sharp fragrance of myrrh clung to her. She wanted to step out and tell her story to the Sadducee, but something warned her that this was much bigger than one priest. To believe her meant he would have to reject his idea of God. He was clinging to falsehoods. Wasn't he halfway in the grave already? But shouldn't she risk everything and tell him what had happened to her? Why else would God raise her from the dead if not to witness to everyone?

A hand on her arm urged her gently back.

"He has made everything beautiful in its time," the shopkeeper whispered at her shoulder. The words from the book of Ecclesiastes were so fresh to her, as if she were hearing them for the first time. She smiled and placed her hand on the shopkeeper's arm. Scripture was now so rich in a way she could not have comprehended in her first life.

That was her first life. What should she call this life?

"You are saying I must wait," she replied.

"I am saying get home safely." He pointed down the street.

The priest was red-faced, yelling at the guard with a scarred cheek who had been chasing her. "I dine with Pilate tonight. Tell me your name!"

The guard stood at attention, gaze forward. "Clemens."

Spittle flew from the Sadducee's lips as he spoke, his face inches from the guard's. "Tell me, Clemens, shall I tell him you are the one who let the woman get away?"

"No!" the guard named Clemens replied, his eyes still fixed on the horizon. He looked pale, in fear of death. Whatever the Romans did to citizens who displeased them, it was probably ten times worse for soldiers who failed in their mission.

Shoshan's stomach dropped. If this young guard saw her again, he would show no mercy. He would capture or kill her. It looked like he would be relieved to achieve either outcome.

The priest snapped his ringed fingers and was surrounded by his entourage of wealthy merchants and several Roman officials. Sadducees attracted them, and like wolves, they always seemed to travel in a pack.

"Reports must be made to Pilate. His wife is so high-strung," the priest commanded as he hurried on his way. "These are childish pranks, that is all. Backlash after the crucifixion. Trying to keep a dead man's dream alive. Take care of it, quickly."

Shoshan watched from the shadows of the shop, waiting.

The hours passed slowly. All she could think of was getting home to Antonius. She dreaded the idea of telling him that their daughter had not been returned to life, but maybe she could find words for her experience in heaven. That would be some comfort to him, wouldn't it? He had never put any faith in Jesus, but when he saw Shoshan, alive and whole, she was sure everything would change for him.

Finally, in the west, the sun began to set, a shimmering diadem of gold and pink.

And she stood there, feeling reborn in a body that still carried the faintest memory of paradise. She had lost her baby. But Jesus was doing something wildly unexpected. There would be more to her story. She was sure of it. But it would be without her daughter here in her arms.

How could life be so beautiful and so cruel?

No more thoughts of paradise, she warned herself. She had work to do. God had not revealed what it was, but He did not let a sparrow fall without His consent. How she had loved those words Jesus said! She placed a hand on her chest, remembering His face as He spoke them.

This little sparrow had fallen, but He raised her up again. She had a second chance to live.

But one question remained. Why had He resurrected her?

CHAPTER FOUR

The streets were completely dark when she left the shop. The day's unrest had driven many people indoors, even away from their roofs. There was no music, no sounds of laughter or shared cups. It seemed no one wanted to attract the attention of a Roman guard. Shoshan wished she could find someone who had witnessed Jesus's arrest and ask why the officials executed Him.

Darting from shadow to shadow, Shoshan made her way down the street, watching for the Roman guard who had chased her. What had been the charge against Jesus? Also, she wanted to find those who had witnessed the resurrections. Maybe they would know if there was a pattern to the ones chosen.

Someone emptied dirty bathwater from a window above, the filth splashing on her from the street. Resisting the urge to shout at the person, she clenched her jaw and kept moving. Now her tunic and robe were wet and filthy. At least she wouldn't smell so strongly of myrrh. She only cared about getting home to see Antonius. A little flame of hope burned in her heart. Her memory was blank in some areas, like where she had spent the time between death and resurrection, so perhaps her recollection was also wrong about her baby.

She knew it couldn't be true that her daughter was alive here. But the thought of home, and of Antonius, made her wish that maybe, just maybe, she had been wrong. Her memories had been so jumbled at first, hadn't they?

Hurrying along toward the southern end of the city, she darted through residential areas, bewildered by the broken stones that she found in the streets, the gaps in the walls where stones had fallen. No earthquake had ever hit the city before, not in her lifetime. God had shaken Jerusalem to its very foundation.

She noticed that lamps burned outside the doorway of every home, even though families had taken refuge from the streets. That seemed odd. Every home signaled that visitors were welcome at any hour.

Her heart skipped as the realization sank in. People throughout the city had heard of the resurrections! Even those who did not attend synagogue and those who mocked Jesus's followers grieved a loss. These families did not hope for another routine visitor. The lamps burned at every doorway in case their loved ones were raised too.

Turning down a narrow street, she heard someone slowly pluck at a lyre. The strings echoed in the street, the notes wavering before fading away. This city had never been so quiet. It was as if everyone held their breath and waited.

As she got closer to her little street, her heart began racing faster than her thoughts. Would Antonius rejoice and weep to see her? Would he cover her face with kisses? Fear began to seize her body, making her stomach turn.

They had been growing apart ever since she announced her pregnancy. She did not understand. Every man wanted to be a father. To have many sons was the dream for Jew and Roman alike.

Maybe when he saw her again, after he had suffered her death and spent days grieving for her, the shock of happiness would overwhelm him and he'd weep. *We will hold each other and weep, yes!* That was what would happen. She would tell him their daughter was alive but in heaven. The tears would come for what they lost, but they had not lost hope. Shoshan would testify to that.

Had the Lord resurrected her for this reason? To soften a man who had so much to offer, to heal a troubled soul? And, she admitted, a troubled marriage. Antonius had not been the best man suited for her. She knew that, but his brooding silence had been a comfort. She had not wanted to reveal all her weakness, not in the early years of their marriage. Too much of her heart had been shattered as a child, on the streets of Rome, but that was a story she never revealed, not to anyone. Not Antonius, and not her best friend, Miriam.

Miriam had not even been able to have children. It had been heartbreaking. Miriam's husband spent his time traveling because the house felt so sad. She urged him to, and said it was good for him to stay busy. He had acquired much wealth. When Miriam's husband died suddenly last year, she had been so stricken with grief that she refused to allow Shoshan to help her prepare the body for burial. No one was allowed to touch him except Miriam. How it broke Shoshan's heart.

But while he was alive, Antonius envied him intensely. "A man only has so many years of physical strength to earn money," Antonius had lectured Shoshan. "But he can have children into his eighties. Even the priests tell us that."

He had such dreams for the future. He worried that Shoshan distracted him from that because she wanted a family. He wanted wealth. In Rome, a common man could achieve that. He planned to earn enough here to move to Rome. He strove to earn the favor of the Roman guards, often working into any conversation that Shoshan had grown up in Rome. She suspected Antonius regretted marrying a Jewish girl, but she always thought he would forget all that when he held his firstborn child for the first time.

A wave of grief overtook her, and she pressed one hand against her belly, bracing herself against the memory. She wanted to be at home, but would home feel the same? She was separated from her child. Yes, she knew her daughter had not lived, but she also couldn't speak of her in the past tense. She knew that the baby was alive. Somehow, she and the others were a testament to that, like sentinels or criers at the gate, telling the city inhabitants what was just beyond the city walls. She knew that interwoven with her body were strange new threads of eternity. Death was not final.

Would she die again? The thought stopped her in her tracks. Pausing, she stooped down and picked up a rock and struck it sharply against the crook of her elbow. It caused stinging pain, although she lacked the courage to sink the stone deep enough to draw blood.

She wasn't immortal. That was good. This wasn't a body, or a world, she wanted forever. It lacked something, but she couldn't describe what. It was something she remembered but could not put into words, like a dream that was just beyond her reach. But now she had to hurry on. Her old life was waiting. Would Antonius be ready? Was she?

Apprehension shook her body as she turned to her front door.

Why was no lamp burning in the doorway?

She stepped back into the shadows across from her door, needing a moment to think. Why did Antonius not put a lamp out? Had he not heard about the resurrections happening in the garden tombs? The Sadducees wanted everyone to think those were rumors and silly tricks. Was that what Antonius believed? He had always been so hard to convince of anything. Especially the truth about Jesus.

He and Jesus had labored together in Cephas, building houses for the wealthy. Antonius refused to believe Jesus was anything but a simple builder and a very odd man, a man who chose to remain unmarried and did not accumulate wealth. He was everything Antonius was not.

Shoshan bent her head. Where was Jesus? Would He come and find her and explain what had happened?

Steadying her nerves, she counted slowly then walked out of the shadows toward her front door. Hand raised, she started to knock, then caught herself and laughed. This was her house. She was not a visitor.

She placed her hand, palm down, on the old wood door, feeling the familiar grooves in the aged cedar. In the afternoons the door was as red as a poppy and still fragrant after so many years. She pushed the door slowly open. The house was dark. But Antonius never traveled, so he had to be home. He was probably asleep in the bedroom, overtaken by grief.

Frustrated at the total darkness, she needed to think about what to do. If she surprised Antonius, he might scream. That would bring Roman guards. He could even strike her, and that could be fatal. He was a big man, his biceps the size of melons from his work carrying stones across building sites.

A dim glow from the upstairs loft helped her navigate safely. Shoshan slowly walked through the kitchen and sitting area to the stairs, arms out to protect herself from stumbling or hitting a wall if she stepped wrong.

At the top of the stairs, she stopped just before calling out his name. She recognized the sound of Antonius's breathing, the deep waves of slumber. *This is it, the moment I reenter my life.*

A petite cough startled Shoshan, her breath catching in her chest, making her gasp.

"Who's there?" demanded a woman's voice in the darkness. The oil lamp on the bedstand moved wildly as someone picked it up.

"It is me!" Shoshan cried out, moving instinctively toward Antonius's side of the bed. "Your wife, Shoshan!"

CHAPTER FIVE

She could hear someone fumbling to adjust the lamp's flame. With a hiss, the lamp flared up bright and wide, illuminating the entire room. Antonius sat up in bed, rubbing his eyes. Miriam was frozen in horror, staring at Shoshan with eyes wide. Miriam's hands began trembling violently, still holding the lamp. The burnt smell of wick and oil filled the room as oil threatened to spill out.

Shoshan rushed forward to grab the oil lamp. "You are going to catch my house on fire."

Antonius's eyes seemed to clear as she moved closer, and he recoiled violently.

"You are dead!" he yelled. He crawled over Miriam and moved to the other side of the bed, farthest from Shoshan. "I saw you die!"

Miriam's face was pale.

This could not be happening.

"This is a dream. It is not real." Miriam flung her hands over her face, unwilling to see her.

Shoshan saw her wedding band on Miriam's hand. She looked at Antonius, the shock making it impossible to say anything.

Miriam! Her husband had died last year. Old age, the physician told everyone, but Shoshan always wondered why Miriam refused to let anyone help her prepare his body for burial. At the time, Shoshan had blamed grief.

Slowly, carefully, Shoshan stepped backward and walked to the stairs. She'd had it planned out in her mind how their reunion would be. She had worried the shock would be too much for him. How foolish she had been! The shock had been hers.

How could Miriam have done this? How could he?

The lamp now illuminated her every step, but somehow, taking the first one seemed impossible. This room, with its revelations, was overwhelming. She had nowhere to go. Her life was here—or had been. She had given birth in this room.

How could they do this?

Whipping around, she raced back to the bed. Miriam and Antonius were huddled together, whispering. They flinched when Shoshan moved toward them. They seemed to think she was a ghost.

Nothing made sense. This betrayal was too shocking to believe or accept.

Shoshan looked at her hands, turning them over, trying to focus on reality. Nothing today had been normal. But it was real, all of it.

Antonius and Miriam watched her in fascinated horror.

Every line of her hands was as it once was. She was alive, but she remembered her newborn daughter laughing with joy. The woman in the shop was right, however. In this life, newborns don't laugh. And her daughter had looked at her with such *knowing*. Her daughter knew Shoshan was her mother. Shoshan was real, and her memory of her daughter was real, even though her daughter was not alive. Or was she?

There was always a chance the baby survived. Shoshan's memory was not perfect. She had not remembered Antonius as capable of betrayal, or Miriam.

"Where is the baby?" she demanded. Since she hadn't seen a body in the grave, there was a chance her memory was wrong, and she was confused.

Antonius started to speak then stopped. He glanced at Miriam, as if struck helpless. Miriam's lips stretched into a thin line. Something made her agitated. Shoshan could almost see the secrets fighting for control of Miriam's face.

Shoshan licked her lips and then dared to make an offer. Even as the words came out of her mouth, she couldn't believe she was saying them.

"Give me my baby," she said softly. "Give her to me, and then you two can do whatever you want. I will not stand in your way." The words were so distasteful that she could feel her lips snarling.

Miriam sniffed the air. Shoshan knew she still smelled of the grave.

Antonius's eyes narrowed.

"You are a spirit. You are dead," he said evenly. "I command you: leave us and go to where your child is."

Resting her forehead against her palm, she groaned, and they looked at each other in alarm. How could he do such a thing, and how could Miriam?

"Why did you say 'your' child?" Shoshan said abruptly, her mind fighting to remember what was true. "She was ours."

Antonius's brow creased, and he shook his head as if not believing what he was seeing. His hand trembled as he rested it on Miriam's shoulder and whispered something in her ear.

"Spirit, listen to me," Miriam began kindly. "Shoshan died in childbirth—"

"I know I died!" Shoshan snapped, interrupting her. "I was there!"

Miriam's face drained of color again. The situation seemed too much for her.

"Shoshan died before the midwife announced the baby was a girl," Antonius said, but his face was turned away. He wouldn't, or couldn't, look at her. Did he feel grief? Did he even feel shame?

"You could not have known the baby was a girl," Miriam finished for him. "You were dead."

Recoiling, Shoshan stared at her friend. No, former friend. Did Miriam feel any guilt? Maybe what she said was true, but Shoshan did not remember the last moments of her life. She was gone before the midwife announced the gender of the baby, but that did not matter. Shoshan had held her daughter, saw her face, and knew her voice in the... *what to call it?* Heaven? It was a strange word. Jesus had called it paradise, but she struggled to remember and understand what that world was. Egyptians called it the afterlife, but that was inaccurate. Worse than inaccurate, it was misleading. Nothing about that life, and that reality, came after this one. It was a new life and new world, entirely separate. Even if this world had never existed, that one would have. It was independent of Earth. How she knew this, she could not explain. So much of her memory had been sealed up when she returned to her old life. All she had was conviction.

But she had always been so ordinary. It made her resurrection a mystery. Why had God chosen to raise her from the dead? Where was Jesus? Was there a plan, or was her resurrection a mistake? Why bring her back but not her daughter?

"Tell me this." Shoshan held up a hand. "If I died in childbirth, what happened to the baby?"

Antonius looked stricken, sick to his stomach. He turned away, his hand covering his mouth.

"What happened?" Shoshan urged Miriam.

Miriam's chin trembled. "Nothing."

"What happened to my daughter?" Shoshan raised her voice.

"Nothing," Miriam said again, very softly this time. "That is what I am trying to tell you. The midwife panicked, but there was nothing she could do. Your baby was not breathing. She never cried or opened her eyes."

Shoshan took a step backward, numb from shock. The words were foul and evil things and should not ever have been spoken. Not over her child, and not over any child. Too many babies died in childbirth, and the mothers too. *What is wrong with this world?* she wanted to scream. Pressing a hand to her heart as if to quiet it, she wondered why her grief flared so violently and without warning.

"Her eyes are brown," Shoshan whispered to herself, then looked at Miriam. "I heard my daughter laughing, Miriam. She is alive."

Antonius looked at Shoshan, his eyes rimmed with red. "What must I bring you?"

"What?" Shoshan could feel her forehead wrinkling as she jerked her head back.

"The baby is buried in the same cave, but farther back, to keep it safe from predators. I can ask the gardener to place an offering with the body," Antonius offered. "Then you will be at peace, yes? You can return to Hades."

Antonius's offer stunned her.

"I am not dead!" Shoshan protested. "And our daughter is alive. I have seen her! She is in the afterlife, and it is nothing like the Romans describe."

The scowl of doubt on Antonius's face infuriated her. How was this ridiculous situation even real? They did not believe she was alive, and she could not believe they had betrayed her.

Since she had woken in this life, Shoshan had been aware of the beauty and artistry of this world, even if it was a poor substitute for the real one, the world her daughter laughed in. Death had destroyed a work of art, and now no one seemed to realize this was not at all what the original was meant to look like.

Looking back and forth between Antonius and Miriam, Shoshan realized they were not going to accept the truth. Dawn was near, and Shoshan had been alive and on the run for hours.

"I am hungry. I would like breakfast," Shoshan announced suddenly. "And my ring back."

Holding out one hand, she waited while Miriam struggled to remove the wedding ring from her own finger. It slid off, finally, and she leaned forward tentatively before quickly dropping it in Shoshan's palm.

With that, Shoshan walked down the stairs and sat at the kitchen table. Hunger, ravenous as the darkness outside, now demanded all her attention, and her body ached with weariness. In a blink, she remembered the struggles of being human, the constant tending of the body, how emotions could flare without warning and disappear just as quickly.

Miriam worked sullenly, assembling a bowl of roasted lamb that had a gray tint, along with wrinkled olives and a scrap of yesterday's bread. Shoshan stared at the bowl and sighed. Miriam had never been a woman who cared about proper household management. She clearly had no interest in offering hospitality to guests either. How had Antonius fallen for her? He had never been kind to people who did not rise to their stations.

No, it was not possible that they were a couple. It was a misunderstanding. She had only been dead for eight days, not even two whole weeks. Antonius had very high standards for behavior. He had to. If he ever hoped to advance in the Roman political world, he had to remember that crimes like adultery were punishable by death. The Romans loved punishing people for their sins.

She did not understand her husband's obsession with winning their favor. Her brother Marcus was the same way. Of course, her brother had succeeded, but it had been years since he wanted to see her.

"It does not look good?" Miriam asked, hands clasped at her chest.

Startled, Shoshan realized Miriam was talking about the food. "I am sure it will be delicious. I have not eaten in…well, since you buried me."

Miriam pressed a hand to her mouth, as if she felt sick. Antonius appeared in the doorway, and she ran to him, cowering at his side.

"Get rid of her, Antonius," Miriam pleaded. "She is here to torment us for what we did!"

Shoshan took a bite of bread, and the crackle of the crust breaking echoed in the silence. She was too hungry to explain anything else without eating breakfast first.

They still thought she was a ghost, which might have been funny to her two weeks ago. But a great sadness filled her now, and seemed to fill the room. She glanced at them to see if they could feel it too, but they just continued to stare at her in fear and dread.

She was sure of what she felt though. A deep, brooding sadness hovered like fog in the streets on a cold fall morning. Shoshan extended her hands without thinking, wishing she could embrace this feeling, for this mourning was somehow a part of God. She sensed that God was sad at a wife deceived, and two people trapped in their lies. God seemed to be very near Jerusalem right now, as if He were looking in the windows, walking in the shadows, sitting by the fires…And as she waited, she had the distinct impression of a holy stillness, every muscle tensing, like when a lion was about to burst from the thicket. Something was coming. A dam was about to burst in her life. But Jesus had risen, that is what the shopkeeper had said. What more could possibly happen?

How do I know this? Ever since she woke in darkness, she had felt the Spirit around her and in this world. She had never felt the Spirit before. He was active, present, in every room, in every moment. And right now, the Spirit was a spirit of grief. Shoshan paused, letting the grief fill her. To feel what the Spirit felt, this was somehow a part of this new life. Miriam and Antonius were not even aware that the Spirit was in the room!

Shoshan wondered if her new life would always be like this, so radically different from her first life, that she would be misunderstood by other people.

Except for the others like her, living resurrected lives. They would understand, she was sure of it. This new life was vastly different. She might still be the same person, but she was so much more. Life too was so much more.

Her gaze flew up, and she stared at Antonius and Miriam. Somehow, she knew now they had done terrible things, even if she hadn't worked everything out yet. She wasn't sure she wanted the details. And she didn't want to press them, because they didn't believe that she had been resurrected. There was a wall between her and them, and she wasn't sure how to overcome it.

They hadn't heard about the others who were resurrected, she was certain. Which meant they hadn't heard about Jesus. They had been huddled together in this house, in their deceit, and had missed the greatest miracle in history.

CHAPTER SIX

S he set her spoon down and fixed her gaze on both.
"Antonius, Miriam, you have to listen to me."

Antonius's jaw flexed, and he wrapped an arm protectively around Miriam. Shoshan glanced down, refusing to feel humiliated. There was something more important.

"You have heard that Jesus was crucified, yes?" she asked. "And that He was resurrected?"

Miriam glanced up at Antonius as if to ask permission then nodded yes. Miriam had walked with Shoshan to hear Jesus teach. She liked Him very much but had seemed reluctant to trust Him with her heart. Now Shoshan understood why. Miriam had already given it to Antonius.

"Do you know how much trouble that man caused?" Antonius snapped. "This city is lucky that Rome did not send a legion of soldiers here to regain order after He overturned the tables at the temple. The streets ran wild with merchants demanding justice!"

"Antonius!" Shoshan raised her voice. "He never asked the people to rebel against Rome. He did not even talk about Rome, or any government, much at all. But think back. Do you remember who He said He was?"

"The exact representation of God," Miriam said under her breath, looking at her feet. "God in the flesh. The Son of God."

"Oh, Miriam, if you know all these things, why do you not know Him?" Shoshan asked. She couldn't hide her disappointment and sorrow.

Miriam's head jerked up then, and the pain in her eyes was indescribable. She was trapped by her sin. Shoshan saw that it wasn't a wall that stood between them. It was a prison door. Shoshan was the only free person in the room.

But there was something more in Miriam's expression, a terrible grief. Shoshan paused then looked again. Miriam had been so curious about Jesus, never able to commit but always wanting to know more. Shoshan groaned with growing suspicion.

"Miriam, when He was crucified, where were you? You watched from a distance, did you not?"

A teardrop stained the kitchen floor at Miriam's feet as she hung her head again, refusing to speak. Then another fell, and another, and the only sound in the kitchen was the soft fall of teardrops hitting the sandy floor.

"What did you see, Miriam?" Shoshan pressed.

"He cried out to His Father, and the earth shook," Miriam said, her voice hoarse. "Have you ever heard a rock split, a rock so large that it is bigger than any man, and the split so large that you could put your entire hand in it? Now imagine that sound from every direction." Her breathing became labored. "It was as if the earth were alive, and it grieved."

The silence was heavy in the room as Shoshan and Antonius waited for Miriam to speak again. Her swallows were audible as she fought emotions.

"I was there," Miriam said finally. "I saw Him die. It is over."

"Miriam, He is not dead anymore! He is risen," Shoshan said, and she could feel joy tugging at the corners of her mouth. "He was the first one resurrected. The others like me, we did not come out until He had. Jesus is alive."

Here, in this room with her betrayers, this house where she had died eight days ago and lost her child, right here, she felt the beginning of joy. It was unbelievable, but this was her resurrected life. The resurrected life was filled with impossibilities, she was discovering.

"If He is alive, where is He?" Miriam moved away from Antonius, who dropped his arm, with a startled and unhappy look on his face.

"I do not know," Shoshan confessed. "But judging from what the other resurrected ones have seen and heard, He is appearing throughout the city."

At some point, she had to stop questioning how things could be and begin asking what she should do in response. It was the only way to stay sane today, perhaps.

"Do you think He would be willing to see me, after all I have done?" Miriam asked.

Shoshan bit her lip. Of course He would. But Miriam had hurt her so badly. Did she deserve to see Him? He would be so tender with her. Shoshan knew it. Did Miriam even have the right to such tenderness? After all, Miriam hadn't even asked her for forgiveness yet. And maybe she never would. Still, Jesus would welcome her.

"Yes," Shoshan said. "Go now and find the disciples. They may know more. But do not tell anyone else what you are doing, or draw attention to yourself. It is not safe."

Miriam did not hesitate. She strode out of the kitchen without saying another word to either.

"Miriam, wait!" Antonius called, but Miriam acted as if she hadn't heard.

Shoshan resisted the temptation to gloat as she watched Antonius. She wrestled with the temptation to lash out in her bitterness. She'd forgotten the slick and rancid taste bitterness left in her mouth.

Even after being in paradise, however briefly, Shoshan was surprised by the intensity of her emotions, including her grief over being separated from her daughter and her anger at Antonius and Miriam. She felt so many emotions, sometimes all at once, and her feelings seemed to spill out before she caught herself.

I know I should want Miriam to find Jesus. An encounter with Jesus would almost certainly lead her to repent. Miriam had to see how badly this betrayal stung. *But perhaps I just wanted her out of my home. God, help. I do not know how to forgive this.*

Antonius leaned over the table, palms spread flat.

"Do you think she really wants to see Jesus?" he sneered, his eyes wandering over her face and frame. "I think she just wanted to get away from you. You are unnatural."

She pressed her lips together, refusing to respond.

"And you stink of death," he added.

Resting her face in her hands, she felt tears building.

"What happened?" she asked. "To you? To us? All I wanted was to come home and be with you, and I find Miriam in our bed, wearing my ring!"

Doubts plagued her now. Did Jesus know this would happen? Was she sure He meant to raise her, or had it been an accident? This just couldn't be how her new life was supposed to unfold.

Antonius wasn't finished. "Tell me, if you really died and were in paradise, why did God not make you perfect before sending you back? You seem like the same woman you have always been, naive and simpleminded. Is there anything different about you?"

"I do not have a husband anymore," Shoshan replied weakly, her heart seared by his words. If she started crying now, though, she felt as if she might never stop. But she needed information from him. She still did not know how she died, not specifically.

"What will you do now?" he asked, folding his arms.

"This is my home," she replied, stunned at the unspoken assumption.

He looked stricken. Clearly, with her gone, he had immediately planned his new life, a life without her. *Or did his planning begin much earlier?* A chill ran down her spine.

Shoshan could not return to the streets. The guards would find her and arrest her. Roman jails were not for holding prisoners until trials. They were for holding prisoners only until the executioner could dispatch them. Sometimes, the executioner never had the satisfaction. If a family did not provide food, the prisoner starved.

Antonius began to grin, and an uneasy feeling settled over her.

"You cannot go out there, can you? They hated Jesus." Antonius picked up the clay pitcher that sat on the table and poured a cup of wine then downed it in one gulp. He wiped his mouth with the back of his hand, eyes glittering as he considered her. "Even the disciples scattered. You are alone in the world."

Had she loved him once? Yes. But that had been a different man. Or was this the real Antonius all along?

"Where were you when He was crucified?" she asked.

"Where do you think?" He smirked. He mimed the action of a hammer driving in nails. "I escorted Miriam to and from, just to keep her safe."

Her blood ran cold. He had been there, watching and cheering, she knew. He had hated Jesus.

But Jesus had changed her so completely. And then she understood why he hated Him. Jesus had given her freedom in her soul, and Antonius could not stop that.

"You liked seeing Him die?" she asked, the sorrow piercing her heart. "Did you rejoice at my death too? Antonius, did you murder me?"

His knees buckled, and he lurched forward. "You must never make that accusation." His eyes darted side to side, even though they were alone. Murder was punishable by death.

"You died in childbirth," he said, and immediately his demeanor changed. Taking a seat opposite her at the table, he lowered his head.

"I lost both of you. Our daughter was beautiful." His voice was the whimper of a wounded child. He reached a hand to her, holding his palm out, waiting for her to grasp hold of it. "I lost my senses from grief. I have done things you hate me for now."

His strength had always affected her. But whenever he let his guard down, she melted. To be the one woman who was allowed to see him when he was vulnerable, how that had moved her.

But had she ever seen the real Antonius?

"I do not hate you, Antonius. I do not know you well enough to hate you." Shoshan took his hand and watched him carefully, hesitating. Here was a faint trace of the old Antonius, the man she fell in love with long ago.

Was it all an act?

"Maybe I buried you alive, by accident?" Antonius said, his voice soft. "After our daughter was born and did not breathe, my judgment might have been clouded."

"Antonius, no."

He jumped up. "I will call for a doctor. This needs to be investigated." He fled from the house.

Shoshan sat at the table, marveling at the morning. So many revelations, none of them pleasant. Was it only two weeks ago that she had stood in this very kitchen, pregnant, excited about the baby, about all she was learning from Jesus? Her whole life was ahead of her, and it was incredibly rich, and getting richer.

Now that life was gone. She had a second life, superimposed almost, on top. Her first life had been full of plans and dreams. But this new, second life? It was a mystery to everyone, most of all herself. What should she do with it? How was she to live?

CHAPTER SEVEN

As the sun set, Shoshan climbed into bed in her empty house. It was her second night in the house, and Antonius was still gone. He had not returned since he left to fetch a doctor yesterday. He probably went to chase after Miriam, she knew. It was Miriam he wanted, not her.

As she sat in bed, looking around the little room, Shoshan's old life echoed all around her, the life she almost had. Again and again, she revisited the memory of holding her daughter, but it did not always remove the sting of living now without her. What did that mean? Was Shoshan losing faith? Or did life here, even a resurrected life, come at a cost? It was hard to bear the truth, but her resurrection hadn't changed the reality of sin.

Still, with Antonius gone, Shoshan was grateful for a moment to breathe and think about what to do next. The familiarity of her home was no longer comforting. The walls closed in. She peered out the window during the day, wishing she could walk on the street or go to the market, or see old friends. But the sight of bloodred plumes on the helmets of Roman guards caused adrenaline to shoot through her body, and she stepped back into the shadows of her home again and again. At night, she didn't dare light an oil lamp for fear the neighbors would ask questions.

Where was Antonius? Who was he talking to? She began to fear that he would come barging through the door at any moment, guards in tow, pointing her out to them. The religious leaders had never liked Jesus, that was true, but if the Roman guards were hunting these resurrected ones, that meant that even Rome did not want rumors spreading.

And of course she knew why.

The Roman emperor, Tiberius, was deeply superstitious. He never took any action without consulting his personal astrologer, and at all times he kept his pet snake at his side, even while traveling. He and his people believed snakes mediated the gap between Hades and the living. Tiberius probably hoped that his snake might be able to take a message to the underworld if needed. If it wasn't so ridiculous to her now, Shoshan would laugh. The image of a snake trying to carry a sealed parchment was the stuff of children's tales.

But two weeks ago, Shoshan would have laughed at anyone wandering through the streets who claimed to have walked out of a grave. Thinking of that, she spotted pale earth under her fingernails, wondering if it was limestone from her tomb, or from the stone that had sealed it.

Tiberius, she reminded herself, might be her biggest problem now, not Antonius. His augurs, who read the natural world for signs, kept sacred chickens who foretold the future by how fast or slow they ate their feed. The Roman Empire was held together by a man who made decisions based on a chicken's appetite. The men lower in the ranks had more sense, and more responsibility. They had to stomp out the rumors of common folk rising from the dead without any apparent incantations or rituals. Otherwise, Emperor Tiberius might do something drastic and unpredictable. The guards would be on alert to catch these resurrected ones and get them off the street before Tiberius heard of them.

So much of this anger toward the believers was driven by fear, and Tiberius had only deepened that anxiety.

Wiggling farther down into bed, Shoshan closed her eyes, hoping to dream of her one remaining memory in heaven. It was all she had to make this world bearable.

Was it seconds later, or hours, that she became aware of men's voices in the house? Warm, gentle fingertips pressed against her neck. Her eyes fluttered open, and she sat upright.

"Pulse is excellent," a man said.

Antonius and another man, much older, stood at the bedside. The man wore a plain brown tunic. A wooden box rested on the bed before him. It was open, revealing its contents: twine, gauze bandages, small surgical knives, clay jars of medicine.

Antonius had brought a physician. Shoshan was stunned. Was Antonius trying to help? Maybe he had been sincere.

The man rummaged through the box and retrieved a jar.

Breathing a small sigh of relief, she studied his face while he worked. He was deeply wrinkled, sunburned across the bridge of his nose, with white eyebrows and a thick white beard. His eyes narrowed as he studied her, but in genuine concern and curiosity, not in a way that left her uneasy. She wondered if he was a retired military physician. His bearing was noble, and he seemed confident, his movements efficient.

"Maybe the midwife made a mistake," the physician said to Antonius. "Who did you hire? I will consult her."

They had been in discussion about her death and resurrection, she guessed.

"I… I cannot really remember," Antonius fumbled his reply. "She was not anyone the neighbors would know either."

The physician stood upright, one eyebrow cocked. He skewered Antonius with a look.

"It was Passover." Antonius shrugged. "You know how the streets are. I could not get to our regular midwife."

It was a good excuse. At Passover, hundreds of thousands of pilgrims flooded the streets of Jerusalem, making the shortest of walks difficult. Had Antonius always been this slippery? she wondered. But then, he was telling the truth about Passover. Maybe it was the cleverest sort of lie, one tucked inside a few facts.

"But even now, the little blood vessels in her eyes are bright red," the physician said, pointing at her face. "Have you noticed? This is common when people have struggled for air."

"As long as my wife recovers fully, that is the important thing." Antonius smiled, immediately dismissing the doctor's question.

"Is it?" the physician murmured to himself. "I should wonder if the most important thing is that she stays well." At this, he glared at Antonius again.

The physician turned and handed the jar of medicine to her.

"I want you to drink two to three sips of this every day. It will give you strength," he urged her quietly. "But prepare your own food and drink. Do not let anyone else do that."

"Why?" she asked.

A wave of sorrow passed over his face. "Humor an old man and do as I say."

"Since the child died at birth," Antonius said abruptly, "some of our friends thought she might have wanted to join her in the underworld. Maybe she did this intentionally."

The physician moved and stood very close to him. Although an old man, he was clearly not intimidated.

"A woman who suffocated herself. Fascinating theory," he replied. "I am sure the Roman courts would love it."

Holding out his hand, palm up, he waited without another word.

Antonius averted his eyes and fished in his money bag on his belt before dropping a coin in the physician's palm.

Shoshan saw that his hand trembled as he paid the physician.

———————

Downstairs in the kitchen, Antonius heated water for a bath after the physician left. Watching him, her back pressed against the doorframe, Shoshan was eager for him to finish. She wanted to wear her own clothes and did not want to put her tunic and robe on until the smell of myrrh, the smell of the grave, was gone. She was alive, even if she had no idea why. Not yet. Surely God would reveal everything to her.

Was she supposed to do something? Should she go into the streets and look for Jesus? The shopkeeper said He was appearing to His followers. That seemed hardly credible, but so much of His ministry had been hard to believe and yet she'd seen much of it herself. And even now, she was tempted to doubt what she had seen.

She had been there for His miracles. Not all of them, of course. Many of them had been done too far north, in Capernaum or the Sea of Galilee. She had not been allowed to travel that far, but the news of the miracles traveled faster than the winds. Healing a blind man, raising a dead girl, casting out the affliction of demons? This was the stuff of legend, and yet the impossible stories were real. The impossible had bowed before Jesus.

Shoshan had thought she would follow Jesus and His ministry forever.

But then came the uproar in the streets of Jerusalem over Jesus and Timaeus. Shoshan and Antonius knew Timaeus's family well and had always grieved for their heartache. Timaeus was their only child and had been born blind. Despite the cruelty of the world, Timaeus was a kind boy who had grown to be a good man.

But it was customs and laws that doomed the family, not his blindness. The rabbis taught that if a father did not train up his son in the family profession, it was as if the father had abandoned the boy as unwanted or unworthy. But how could a stonemason train a blind son? He could not. To many in the city, Timaeus's blindness, and the fact that he begged for coins at the city gate, was a condemnation of his father.

The father did not want any more children after Timaeus's birth, and the mother lived with her broken heart. She loved Timaeus and knew that if he had not been born blind, she would have had a different life. The whole family would have. But still, they attended synagogue and temple faithfully. They tithed, sang, and celebrated the festivals. They forgave the gossip and focused on their God. Nothing ever changed for them except the seasons.

Shoshan had been in the market buying roasted chickpeas when she heard the uproar. She dropped her basket and ran when she heard that Jesus had spit on Timaeus. What she saw defied explanation. Timaeus's eyes were covered with mud.

"Go wash in the Pool of Siloam," Jesus said.

This was the pool that the priests used for ritual baths before entering the temple. Shoshan heard the crowd's furious clamor. Jesus had spit in the dirt to make mud then smeared it on Timaeus's eyes. Timaeus was now unclean. And the indignity!

Timaeus's mother shoved her way through the crowd, taking hold of his hand. When Shoshan last glimpsed them, they were walking in the direction of the pool, the mother leading her son. Soon after that, the streets were wild with the news. Timaeus could see. His sight was fully restored after he washed his eyes.

The miracle tore the synagogue apart. Timaeus and his family were forced to decide: renounce the miracle and Jesus, or renounce their community.

A rabbi had stopped by Shoshan's house a few days later. He wanted to know what Shoshan had seen, since she was a known follower. How had Jesus performed this magic trick? he had demanded.

She tried to explain it was not magic but miracle. And, she pointed out, trying to be helpful, that God made man from the dust of the earth. Why couldn't the Son of God create from dust too?

The rabbi warned Antonius to keep her under his watch more carefully, or there would be consequences. The warning was clear. Antonius would lose jobs. He might be the next man at the gate begging for coins.

Antonius had been furious. For him, that was the moment he decided to hate Jesus.

"Your prophet could destroy that family!" Antonius raged. "He is bringing chaos to everything He touches!"

It was true, in its way, and Shoshan did not reply. Their son could see, but the parents were at risk of losing their place in the synagogue. They would lose their friends, business contacts, financial standing, access to trade, reputation. They would lose everything they valued in this life in exchange for their blind son regaining his sight.

To Antonius, that was unforgivable, a bargain he would never make.

Now, looking back at that moment, Shoshan wondered why she hadn't seen Antonius right then for the man he was. Maybe she had and didn't want to admit it. Was that the reason she sneaked out to listen to Jesus, even following Him as far as Bethany? And when Jesus raised Lazarus from a tomb, Shoshan had nearly fainted from shock. Coming home, she hadn't been able to speak of it with Antonius. She knew of a resurrection and could not share the news with her husband. It had been excruciating. She had prayed for a way to speak of it, to share the news, to convince Antonius of the truth about Jesus and His ability to resurrect the dead.

Now, stretching her arms overhead as she shimmied out of her tunic, Shoshan laughed out loud.

Thank You for the answered prayer. The tunic's gauze passed over her eyes, and for a moment, the world looked soft. Her breathing echoed in her ears. Flinging the gown to the floor, she caught sight of her hands.

Here was the evidence of her words. Standing in the kitchen, dirt from the grave under her fingernails, yet Antonius did not believe. He had put her in the tomb himself! Maybe he had even killed her himself.

She could not convince him. No one could. She had to stop trying and start concentrating on what to do next. Was she in danger if she stayed in her own home? What did God expect her to do, if not return home? *Lord, what now?*

"Come." Antonius crossed his arms. "The water is ready."

CHAPTER EIGHT

Soaking in the cramped tub, her knees pushed nearly to her nose, Shoshan tried to let the water relax her muscles. Antonius set a plate of washing ash next to her on the side table with a linen cloth. A jar of bath oil was nestled alongside the cloth.

He opened the jar, poured a steady stream onto the cloth, and moved behind her. She sat up higher in the water as he placed the cloth on her right shoulder and rubbed. The fragrance of lavender enveloped the room.

"This has all been such a shock," he said. She could not see his eyes or detect his mood by the tone of his voice. It sounded as if he was trying to make peace with her.

He wiped the bath oil on her left shoulder then placed the cloth on the table. Both hands went around her neck, and her breath caught in her chest. His hands moved to her shoulders, kneading her muscles. The skin along her arms prickled.

"What happened after you woke up?" he asked, emphasizing his choice of words.

But she had not simply fallen asleep inside the grave.

"Do you mean after I was resurrected?" she replied.

"Yes, that," he replied pleasantly. He spoke to her as if she was recalling a dream, nothing more. "What did you do? Tell me about it."

As best she could, she told him what she had experienced from the moment her eyes fluttered open. Walking in the fish market, then navigating the streets with people in an uproar and the guards trying to keep the peace. She left out the part about hiding in the codex shop. There was no need for Antonius to know about that shop or its owner, or that the resurrected ones had hidden there. They still might be meeting there, in fact.

"The guards were looking for you?" Antonius perked up.

Too late, she suspected that Antonius saw her predicament not as a threat to her life but an opportunity.

"I should go out and get food," Antonius said, abruptly changing the conversation. "You are in no condition to cook for us."

Before she could even reply, he grabbed her tunic draped over the chair and left. He had just returned, and now he was gone again. This time, she suspected, he would not stay gone. Without meaning to, she'd given him a way to get rid of her permanently.

Heart pounding, Shoshan knew he was not going to get food. He even took her tunic, intending to leave her naked and helpless. It was a careless mistake, to think that the loss of one tunic was enough to trap her here. He had taken the tunic he had buried her in, but she had another. In his panic, he might have forgotten about it.

Unfolding herself from the tub, dripping on the floor, she rushed to the bedroom and pulled the basket of linens from underneath her bedside table. Her everyday tunic was not there, or her robe, and her heart sank at the loss.

Instead of her own belongings, Miriam's clothes sat in the basket. Irritated by the discovery, Shoshan recognized the fine weave of linen right away. Miriam indulged herself with material possessions after her husband died, and she liked gaudy colors and fine fabrics. The clothes smelled of Miriam's perfume, a cassia blend Shoshan disliked. Shoshan dressed quickly, wincing at the cloying fragrance that cut through the heady floral notes of the bath. At least the clothes were good quality and would not draw attention.

At the front door, she peeked carefully from side to side, watching for any sight of Antonius or the red feather plume of a Roman guard's helmet. Where could she go? The shopkeeper might not welcome her back, not with the guards patrolling to stamp out the rumors of resurrected ones in the streets. There was one other home in Jerusalem where they might open the gates for her, even now. But she could not bring herself to entertain the idea of that. The humiliation would be too great.

There was only one place she could go where Antonius would not think to look for her.

Stepping out, she blended into the people on the street, pulling her veil low, hoping no one would recognize her. She had to get away before Antonius brought the guards there to arrest her. She paused, looking back at her home, knowing she might never return.

She was a forsaken woman in the city of God, and now she was on the run.

As she moved through the streets, she was surrounded by crowds. Everyone was reluctant to go indoors. Maybe some still watched, hopefully, for a loved one to return from the grave. She overheard bits of gossip about the events of the past week. Some claimed to have seen Jesus strolling down the same road that He had walked to the cross.

"He seemed quite healthy, and perfectly cheerful," one man said.

"He even passed the same guard who whipped Him with the cat o'nine tails," another added, "and He was not angry. The guard must not have recognized Him. But if Jesus really had the power of God, of course, He would have struck that man down where he stood. Can you imagine, whipping the Son of God? God would punish that. Jesus did not understand the fury of a righteous God."

There was much clucking and murmuring, as if these men knew the truth of it all.

"It was all quite a trick," the first man insisted. "Just like pretending to raise His good friend Lazarus from the dead. Jesus was the best magician Jerusalem had ever seen. The emperor would pay a fortune to see how He did these marvels!"

Shoshan gritted her teeth to keep herself from jumping into the conversation and rebuking the men. Why wasn't she used to these comments by now? Jesus had done so many good things for the people, and yet there was always someone who said the vilest things about Him. And His followers, she remembered. She had heard those rumors too, that His followers drank blood and ate human flesh and exploded in violence whenever they entered the sacred temple grounds. The followers of Jesus, the rumors went, were dangerous cultists to be avoided.

And yet Shoshan knew, because she had seen it, that if any of these families had a sick child and medicine was unable to heal them, the parents had rushed to Jesus, pleading or even demanding help and deliverance.

What would these people do now, she wondered? Were they more frightened of a Jesus who had been crucified and buried, or a Jesus they could no longer find?

Keeping her veil low, she raced against the sun as it slipped farther down. She nimbly passed through the crowds along the western side of the city and then approached the Essene Gate. Pausing to look behind her at the beloved city, she saw the temple far to her right in the distance, the evening shadows softening its edges. Just beyond that, to the right, was the Mount of Olives. She had heard such wonderful teachings there.

Looking down, she fought tears as her throat tightened. She had once felt so protected inside these walls. Now nothing was certain.

Who would have ever guessed that Jesus's ministry would come to this? He had been tortured, and crucified on a cross to die in a public display, a warning to any citizen who might dare make similar claims.

No one ever had. No one ever claimed to be the fulfillment of all law and prophecy. No one ever did such miracles.

Shoshan looked directly over to the Tomb of David, so close to the palace of the high priest. Such strange neighbors in these times. What would David have thought of his city now? What would he have done if he had seen the King of the Jews stripped and beaten, paraded through these streets to be crucified? David had danced over the stones to welcome the ark of the covenant! Those very stones were stained now with the blood of God.

Glancing at the sun, she decided to risk a delay.

She walked to his tomb and rested a hand on the stone inscribed with his name. David had loved this city so very much. He had instructed Solomon how to build the first temple, giving him detailed instructions, plans, and measurements. David's life was poured into this city. Then came the Babylonians, and the temple was destroyed. The ark disappeared. When Herod the Great rebuilt the temple, he did not follow David's plans and measurements, the ones received from the Lord. Herod fashioned the temple as seemed best to him. She wished she could have seen the temple that Solomon had designed from the plans David gave him.

Shoshan looked up at the temple, the setting sun illuminating the western wall in bands of orange and gold. It was beautiful in its way. The city itself was lovely. Jerusalem, beloved city of David and the eternal King. *If only you had known!*

She felt a hand on her shoulder, comforting and warm. Lifting her face with a gasp of relief, recognizing the touch, she looked around in confusion. Wasn't the Teacher here? She felt His touch on her shoulder, comforting her. Or maybe that was her imagination, because as she glanced from side to side, He was not there. People were milling around, going in and out of the gate, hurrying to get home or get out of the city before the gates closed for the Sabbath.

She picked up the edge of her robe and joined the foreigners and pilgrims leaving Jerusalem. Pausing at the Essene Gate, she looked back. She had already left her home and her marriage. Now she was leaving her beloved city, Jerusalem.

Would she ever be able to return?

CHAPTER NINE

The soldier in charge at Essene Gate looked at her sternly. "You are going out? Before sunset?" He seemed surprised.

She nodded.

"You are new to our city, yes?" he asked.

She bristled at his use of "our." Jerusalem did not belong to Rome. It never would.

"Yes." She furrowed her brow and tugged at her veil. "You must be very smart to see that so quickly."

Antonius had always flattered people. She could try it.

"If you are new to the city, you need to know that Sabbath begins tonight. The priests at the temple will blow a shofar late in the afternoon, before the sun sets, to warn everyone. You must finish your business and hurry home. Once the sun sets, Sabbath begins and this city is dead. Not a soul stirs. No market is open. No food or drink sold anywhere for any price. Make sure your mistress has whatever she needs before sunset, do you understand?"

"Sounds dreadful," she lied. It was peaceful. Or had been, back in the days when she had a little home and friends and family to rest with. She could not bear the thought of sitting still with her broken heart for twenty-four hours right now, these scenes of betrayal replaying in her mind. Why hadn't God done away with her hurts and pains from the old life when she was resurrected? He had given her a new life, but He had not done away with her grievances. Did that mean it was up to her to forgive? Why couldn't He have just wiped away her memory?

There were no answers to be found, however, and she knew that. Instead, she hurried through the Essene Gate. She had to get out of the city before anyone recognized her. If Antonius heard she had been spotted, he would turn her in. Perhaps even now he was inquiring about the reward he might get for tipping off the soldiers to one of these Jesus followers attempting to cause distress in the streets. And distress was the right word—families whose lamps burned but no knock was heard at their door? What heartache. Their sorrow would turn to fierce anger, she knew. Everyone hated death. It never seemed just or fair, not when it came for their loved one.

She climbed up into the graveyards, where there was nothing but quiet and peace. Or there once had been. She saw the evidence of stones overturned at one grave and dirt disturbed. She wondered who this person was, why they had been resurrected and where they had gone. She paused and blessed them in her mind, hoping they were safe in the city tonight.

Graves surrounded Jerusalem. Most were to the north, including Golgotha, where criminals were frequently crucified. Shoshan hid among the tombs and slept for a few hours after the sun set. When she awoke, she sat, thinking of what she should do next.

How fitting that I should return here at this moment when I am confused and scared.

She knew Antonius would never comb through the graveyards looking for her. He didn't believe she had been resurrected. What did he think? Maybe that she had been buried alive, that whatever he had done to her had not worked.

Shoshan knew how frightening it must have been for those who did not believe in Jesus to see the dead returning from all directions, walking into the city. Sometimes miracles only hardened the heart. She knew that firsthand.

And she had not always believed Jesus either. But it was not a miracle that convinced her of His identity, not even Timaeus's miracle. It was an olive tree.

On that day, standing beneath the old olive tree outside the city, listening to Jesus teach, Shoshan had felt the quickening of life in her womb. The trees here had lined the mountains for hundreds of years, maybe more, and the olives were pressed to make the sacred oil for anointing kings. But it was this grove that David had retreated to when betrayed by Absalom. David had been forced to flee the city he loved, and he found refuge in the olive grove, the place that had provided the oil for his anointing. The call of kings had first stirred in this soil. The Lord of heaven had blessed these trees for His mysterious and divine purposes, and it was here that she felt the stirring of life for the first time.

Jesus often prayed here alone—His disciples had told her that. But the teaching that day was a tangle, like the roots of the tree, about truth and pain. His teaching was not an easy thing to accept, and it was not an easy thing to forget.

But that day she watched as He stood under an olive tree, and wondered if this was the tree that would give the oil to anoint Him. When He became King, she would be able to tell her child that she had been here with Him.

She believed He was the Lamb of God. She was not so learned that she wrestled with the old scrolls and their implications or needed to argue about prophecy and law. His words were enough for her. That made her feel slightly ashamed. Antonius always said she was too gullible. But she knew the truth when she heard it.

When she felt the first flutter of life in her womb, Jesus had smiled, meeting her eye, as if He knew. It seemed like this grove and nature, all of it spoke to Him too. All of life was a whisper in His ears.

Now she wondered how such a kind and gentle man had made such terrible enemies. He had been doomed from the start. Had He known that day that her marriage and the baby were doomed too?

The graveyard had always been a quiet place because no one lived there. But not anymore, not since Jesus rose. Life had come to those graves.

Life had come to all of this place. No wonder stones had fallen.

Carefully, she picked her way around the city, staying out of sight, working her way over the hills until she arrived back at her own grave. She had meant to hide in the cemetery but, without any thought, had walked directly back to her own grave. The stone that had sealed the cave was flat on its face in the sandy dirt.

Her stomach dropped. She knew if she went in, she would see her child, her daughter, wrapped in her burial shroud. But she had to see her, had to confirm with her own eyes that her daughter had not been resurrected with her. Otherwise, Shoshan would be haunted by thoughts of her infant alone in a cave. Shoshan had to see the body and know the truth. God had not resurrected her daughter.

She lay down to sleep, and as dawn broke in the east, she awoke and was still unable to go in, the gaping dark hole in the side of the cave taunting her. Her child was in there. If Shoshan walked back in and picked her little body up, what would happen? Was there any chance or hope of resurrection here on earth?

No. Somehow, Shoshan knew her daughter had not been included in the unexplained miracle, and the pain dropped her to her knees, pebbles digging into her skin. Why? Why raise Shoshan but not her daughter?

Why not raise a child, an innocent child? A wave of grief overwhelmed her. Even knowing her daughter was in heaven was not enough to comfort her or hold back the agony.

She felt her heart might split apart, just like the sealing stone in the dirt. Her mind could not hold onto both realities at once. Heaven was real, but so was Earth, and Earth was where Shoshan had to live. She had to live here without her daughter.

Why, O Lord? Why raise me at all?

Shoshan looked around. She knew families who had lost infants in the past few years. None of those graves were open. Was there a more wretched sight on this earth? But she had seen Jesus do miracles and knew He had raised a dead girl to life. She knew He had raised His friend Lazarus. He had the power to raise people from the dead, no matter their age.

Her thoughts turned to the stories she'd heard of Jesus's resurrection. He had been raised too. No matter what had happened to the body, Jesus could bring them back.

A sudden conviction struck her. God had raised her from the grave, and she had not done anything worthy of such a miracle. She did not even have a mission or purpose that could justify such a supernatural intervention.

It was as if God had made a mistake.

She became aware of a mourner who had joined her in the graveyard, a kind-looking man with a weathered face, the grief lines around his eyes so deep Shoshan could have traced the hollows with the tip of her finger. If he recognized her as a resurrected one, he gave no indication. She breathed in relief. His presence was a comfort.

A tear rolled down his cheek as he looked at a closed tomb near her.

"This is a hard thing to see," he said, his voice hoarse with emotion.

"Yes," she replied, grateful for the company.

"I cannot make sense of it," she said. Stealing a glance at him, she decided to risk telling him a little more and moved toward him. "I know the truth about heaven. But this is truth too. This is just as real."

The man put his hand on her arm. She felt windswept, a fresh breath of life in her lungs, the air after a rain, crisp and clean. It was a wild, pure strength, the way water hit her tongue after a fever. His touch revived her.

"Shoshan," he replied.

Shocked, she turned to look at His face.

"Teacher!" It was Jesus standing next to her.

Why had she not recognized Him at first? His face was transformed looking at her, love beaming from His eyes.

She grabbed Him without thinking, wanting to hug Him, forgetting all that was proper, forgetting even the laws that the rabbis taught, that a woman could not touch a man in public like that.

He laughed and stepped back, placing His hands on her arms to look her directly in the face. His dark brown eyes were so kind and warm, the lines that radiated out as He smiled, showing his absolute delight in her. He held on to her with the hands that had always had such calluses from His years as a builder.

Suddenly she noticed the gaping wounds still present on his lower palms, just at the wrists. She recoiled in horror.

He sighed deeply, lifting them so she could look at them, studying them with her. Their eyes met, and she looked back down, tentatively tracing the outline of the wound on his right palm with the tip of her finger, glancing up every few seconds to be sure it did not hurt Him.

"You do not feel any pain?" she asked.

He shook His head. "I do not have that kind of body anymore."

"But you have the wounds," she replied, confused. "Why keep the wounds?"

If He had a new body, a body that was better in some way than a normal human body, able to do things like rise from the dead and appear to people throughout the city, why would He want to keep the wounds of torture and death?

"What those men did to you!" she said, not waiting for His reply, her anger rising. "I was not there, but I heard. Where were the disciples? Why couldn't they stop it? I would have done something! At least I would have tried."

Jesus held up a hand to silence her. The wound was so large that she could see a bit of light piercing through the other side of his flesh. The nails had been large. She winced and looked away.

"This was My Father's will." His voice was calm. How could He have no anger at all? Shoshan realized she was furious, not just for Jesus but for herself. She had been betrayed too. Worse than the betrayal, she was stuck here, with a second chance at a life but without her daughter and with no idea how to go forward. Nothing was the way it was supposed to be, not for Jesus and not for her, at least not as she understood it.

"Why did You return from the dead?" she asked, gesturing helplessly at the unopened graves all around them.

His face softened with kindness. He must have understood her real question.

Why leave heaven? Why come back to this world of betrayal and death?

He touched her cheek with His thumb, and she realized she had tears on her face.

Overhead, clouds rolled over the sun, casting lazy shadows across the cemetery.

"I said I would," He replied. His face softened into a somber, serious expression. "Look around, Shoshan. Everyone dies. At a certain age, you even expect it. But resurrection is not expected. It is not a natural event. It is supernatural. It is God. It is Me. I am the resurrection."

"But why did You raise others? When You were alive—" She stopped herself. He was alive now, wasn't He? "Before Your death, You raised people, and after Your death, people came out of the tombs. Not everyone, just some people. I do not understand that," Shoshan said. "And why is my body different than Your body?"

She understood why He raised Lazarus. He loved Lazarus. But why her? He had never even spoken to her privately before today. But her resurrected body was very human. She felt physical pain and weakness. Even harsh words hurt.

He didn't seem to experience pain of any kind.

"Go to your brother and tell him about Me," Jesus replied.

Shoshan choked and coughed, caught off guard by the shock. "My brother?"

How did Jesus even know she had a brother? She hadn't spoken to her brother in nearly three years, not since his wedding. Even before then, their relationship was strained. If he was brokenhearted over what had happened to her in Rome, he had a strange way of showing it. He did not just like Rome, he wanted to be a Roman, despite it all. Despite her.

"…Not since he found out you were following Me," Jesus said.

He knew what had happened? Of course He knew.

"You know I cannot. He is close with the Sadducees, after all." She smiled lightly, as if that explained everything. Sadducees probably hated Jesus more than the Pharisees, but it was hard to tell. To a Sadducee, the written law was the entire revelation of God. There could be no revelation or understanding beyond the written word. God was finished revealing Himself.

When Jesus used that same written law to shame the Sadducees for their hardened hearts, they had become enraged. Shoshan had begun to understand that they were worshiping the law, not the God who gave it. Somehow along the way, over many years, rules and codes became their God. They had no love for humanity.

"Did you not once say to yourself that if I asked you to do something, anything, you would do it?" Jesus asked.

She scoffed, blinking rapidly. "But Marcus has been horrid to me." And how did Jesus know her inner thoughts? If He did, then surely He understood why she could never turn up at Marcus's gate, desperate and frightened. Marcus had seen her like that once before, when they were children, and look how he responded.

Cold and arrogant, he was the perfect friend to the Sadducees. He had married the niece of a high priest. A beautiful girl, she had brought great wealth into the marriage, and many political connections. Instantly, Marcus was a member of the ruling class. Like many of them, he was not especially religious, but the Sadducees were the party of the elite.

Marcus regularly dined at the palace of the high priest and entertained the Roman government officials at his home. The last time Shoshan had visited, just as her interest in Jesus became known to Marcus, she had been amazed at the tile work Marcus had installed. The mosaics in the private baths were stunning. His house was bigger than any house she had ever been in.

But he had sold his soul to buy it. If he ever loved God, or Shoshan, he now loved money and influence much more. When Antonius mentioned that Shoshan had followed Jesus to Bethany and witnessed a miracle…

Marcus had been hosting a dinner party. Antonius was anxious to make business contacts and urged Shoshan to talk very little. But someone whispered in Marcus's ear, and he abruptly stood.

Pointing a finger at her, as if she were a plague victim, he ordered his guards to remove her immediately. Everyone stopped eating and drinking. The musicians struck wrong chords as their fingernails grazed the strings of the lyres.

That was it. He did not even say her name. Guards grabbed her by the elbow and yanked her up out of her seat. Antonius, seated at another table, did not follow. She was at home, in bed, her face swollen from tears, before he finally arrived. Even Antonius did not want to be associated with her.

So she was now an embarrassment and a liability to Marcus, the sister who wandered the countryside listening to a cult preacher who encouraged His followers to question the religious leaders and who performed strange magic tricks. That is all His miracles were, the leaders said.

"You have to see him," Jesus said, interrupting her thoughts. "You have to heal."

She would never heal from the past, she knew that. What had happened in Rome was Marcus's fault, and he had never shown her any pity.

How can there be healing when there is no remorse?

CHAPTER TEN

A cool breeze swept past her, and she pulled her robe tighter as she felt her face grow flushed. She had to remember that He seemed to be able to know her thoughts. His resurrected body was so different than hers, but that was one quality she was glad she did not share. She might have died from shame and anger if she had been able to hear the thoughts of Antonius and Miriam. Her own best friend! How could she?

All Shoshan wanted was to hold her baby girl and hear her laugh just one more time.

"I am sorry, I cannot," Shoshan said, backing away. "You know what it is like, being broken and humiliated. Cast out by your own. And my husband betrayed me with my best friend. My mind just keeps going back over the offenses. I do not want this life. I do not think I should have been resurrected. You made a mistake."

"Shoshan."

"I do not want to be here." She grabbed Him by the sleeve. "Let me return to my daughter, please."

"You will," He promised, His face soft with compassion. She felt she could stare into His eyes for hours. They soothed her and made her feel safe in a way she'd never known. "But not today."

"Why was she not resurrected too?" she asked.

"Will you trust me?" His voice was gentle. "With her, your new life, everything?"

Her hand fell from his sleeve, the reality of her situation sinking in. Of all the people who could have been raised to life, people with loving families who would have rejoiced to have them back home, Jesus had chosen her. She had no family to return to. Her daughter would remain in heaven. And her only living relative despised her. *This is the life Jesus wants me to have?*

"No," Jesus replied, but the oddest thing happened. She did not hear His voice with her ears but heard it in her heart. "I want you to *give* this life."

She looked into His eyes again.

"I am afraid," she said. "Marcus does not want anything to do with me. He will say it is my fault that my daughter died and Antonius betrayed me. He will turn me over to the Roman guards. Please do not ask me to do this. You will be sending me to my death."

"You know that death is nothing to be feared," Jesus replied. "You know that I am the resurrection. You know that, Shoshan."

"Last month, if You had asked me to do something for You, anything at all, when I was just one more face in the crowd"—she smiled ruefully—"I would have thought I was the luckiest woman in the world. But now? This is too much. I do not have the strength."

"I do," He answered gently. "Go to Marcus when the Sabbath is over. The streets are not safe, so travel when the sun goes down tonight."

Looking at her Savior, the prophet she had traveled the countryside to see and hear, she knew He was the Son of God, and she knew that His resurrection had disrupted the natural order of this world. She just had never expected that it would disrupt her world so much.

This was not a life she wanted or asked for. This was a life given to her, or thrust upon her, against her wishes. Maybe that was the meaning of resurrection—that the new life would be unrecognizable.

"Will You come with me?" Shoshan pleaded. "I will need more than my testimony. The Sadducees do not believe in the afterlife or resurrection and I…Well, I have nothing in common with him now. He is married. He wants nothing to do with me. I need power to convince him of the truth."

A group of young boys in the cemetery wandered to the tomb where Jesus had been buried. The tallest boy, with ragged clothes and a dirty face, kicked a rock into the darkness of the open cave. The others pretended to scream in fright and cower behind him, as if expecting someone to come charging out.

An elderly man shooed the boys away and looked in it for himself, calling down a curse on the soldiers who let the pranksters get away with the joke.

"I was there," the man announced to anyone who listened. "He was dead—I personally attest to that. And dead He remains, I assure you of that. If I am wrong, may lightning strike me where I stand!"

Jesus and Shoshan turned away, pretending not to listen, but she saw the corners of His mouth twitching with amusement.

A strike of lightning in the distance followed by a low rumble of thunder made the boys run in terror. The man's knees visibly trembled under his tunic as he hurried down the hill.

She looked with alarm at Jesus only to see His shoulders were shaking. His eyes were twinkling with delight.

Laughing behind one hand cupped over her mouth, she felt relieved somehow. Not that this old man had tempted God without knowing it but that Jesus had endured the very worst of humanity and yet still loved everyone. And now He was asking her to do the same.

Closing her eyes, she breathed in and released one last deep breath before nodding her acceptance. "I will do as You have asked."

When she opened her eyes, He was gone.

Marcus lived in the area of Jerusalem known as the Upper City, which was not far from Herod's palace. Shoshan entered Jerusalem through the Women's Gate this time to avoid seeing anyone twice or calling attention to herself. Passing by the temple on her left, she walked until the Upper City was up and to her right.

Her pulse quickened as she walked toward Herod's palace. Many soldiers would be stationed near the palace, and the streets surrounding Herod's Theater would be crowded with revelers.

She slipped silently through the streets, surprising herself at how adept she was becoming at staying in the shadows. For the first time, she paid attention to the others who hid too. She saw the orphans, the sick and homeless, all those who would creep out in the sunlight to wait by the Pool of Miracles. There was a city at night that was entirely different. It felt to her like discovering a new species of animal, one with a different heartbeat, different sounds and smells.

In these streets at night, there was more music but less food. She could smell the acrid scent of cheap lamp oil burning, and hear murmurs from women sitting in the shadows, their babies crying. She watched as young children darted through the marketplace, where the many stalls sat empty, scavenging for crumbs or dropped treasures to sell the next day.

Her gaze followed one young girl who stood alone by an empty cart. The girl's chin trembled as she looked at the ground, and Shoshan guessed there were no more scraps to be found. *The girl is hungry.* Before Shoshan could move toward her, to comfort her if nothing else, a woman sitting in a doorway beckoned to the girl. Lifting her eyes, Shoshan gasped softly.

This was the woman Shoshan met in the codex shop, one of the resurrected ones, the woman who brought bread to Nehemiah's workers. *Why is she living in the street?* The girl approached the woman readily. *They must be familiar to each other.*

The woman reached into a bag at her waist and handed something to the girl. Taking it, the girl sat cross-legged, her back to the woman. Transfixed, Shoshan watched as the woman took one more thing from her bag, a comb. While the girl ate, the woman gently moved the comb through the girl's messy hair. One hand combed, the other smoothed and patted. A moment later, the girl was finished eating and leaned her head into the woman's hand, only briefly, before jumping up and darting away back into the night.

Shoshan approached. "What are you doing here?" Didn't she have a family to return to? But no, they would all be dead by now. The woman had lived so long ago.

The woman's face brightened when her eyes alighted on Shoshan, and she motioned to her with one hand. Shoshan approached, relief and curiosity making it hard to decide what to ask first.

"I do not understand…" Shoshan stammered then smiled and exhaled.

"Several believers, and many good Jewish faithful, supply me with leftover food every night."

That explained how the woman had something to offer the young girl.

"But the comb?" Shoshan asked. Why did the woman comb the girl's hair?

"No one cares for these children," the woman said quietly, out of earshot of anyone else. "They are not only ritually unclean, they are physically dirty. Hair in tangles and knots. Unwashed clothes. How long has it been since they felt a mother's kind touch?"

"You do not care that this makes you unclean too?" The woman could not go to the temple if she was unclean, not unless she had the money to pay for sacrifices. Judging by her appearance, any money she had was spent on these children.

The woman's eyes closed, and she nodded, acknowledging the problem before fixing her gaze on Shoshan again.

"I trust that somehow, God will make me clean in His way and His time. Until then..." her eyes flicked to something just over Shoshan's shoulders.

Shoshan became aware of a little boy hovering a short distance away, watching the woman with a hopeful expression. The woman beckoned the boy to approach, but the child's gaze moved to Shoshan, fear in his eyes.

Blessing the woman, Shoshan moved on, pondering the encounter. The woman had lost so much: her family, friends, and home. Yet she cared for these children, perhaps because they had also lost so much. And she seemed pleased to have a purpose for her new life.

Shoshan had never seen this side of the city, not in fifteen years of living here. She'd always been inside when the sun set, safe and warm, serving a full dinner to her husband, preparing for bed.

God had wanted her to see this woman and the hungry children, she was sure of it. And this other resurrected woman was not really alone in the world. She was now a mother to the children of the streets.

Passing the Essene Gate, she watched as people flooded through the gate. There was always a burst of activity when the gates reopened after Sabbath. Watching them all, she wondered about their lives and if they had anyone to care for them.

Nearby, Shoshan saw people streaming out of Herod's Theater, heads bent together, laughing over what they'd seen. *Which comedy is Herod putting on for the people?* The comedies of Plautus were still in favor. Antonius liked his comedies very much but vastly preferred spectacles that included fighting.

Players in costume, animals, and magicians would be filing out from the back doors soon, she knew. Children loved to catch sight of the animals especially. She'd planned on taking her own child there one day.

Now she had no child, no marriage, no life she recognized. The woman she'd talked to had found a way to make great use of this new life. How would Shoshan do that? Her brother was alive and their relationship still ruined.

What would Marcus say when he saw her? What would she say? Would his wife even allow her through the door or allow her to spend the night? If not, where would Shoshan sleep? Her stomach burned with hunger too. When was the last time she had a good meal? Food at her home hadn't counted. It had been hard to eat in the presence of her betrayers.

The high priest's palace was on her right, but there was another high priest's palace farther down in the city by the tomb of David.

She slipped behind Herod's Theater, hoping to avoid any guards or priests. Pausing for a moment in the shadows, she watched the acrobats stretching and marveled at their abilities. One of the women caught her watching and smiled. The woman gestured to a blanket spread on the ground by the performers. Shoshan peered closely then understood. The woman was offering to share their food and drink.

The woman thought Shoshan was a beggar. Why else would a woman be wandering alone at night?

Heat flooded into her cheeks as she shook her head to decline the offer, but she clasped her hands as she did, hoping the woman would not be offended. She had once avoided them. Now she was so deeply thankful for their kindness. She was an outsider now too, walking among the beggars and scrapers-by, the people who clung to the shadows. She was nothing like them, she wanted to shout. And yet, she was exactly like them now. Alone, hungry, and afraid.

She had never known how quickly life could turn on someone, how a safe, warm bed could be taken away, and how the shadows hid so much of the city.

Shoshan recognized the street. It had taken her too long to get here undetected. Traveling at night had been far more dangerous than she realized. The guards patrolled the streets, looking for agitators.

She had hidden for nearly a whole week before she was able to travel safely, taking shelter in the shadows at first, until a kind woman took her into her home and fed her. The woman was not a believer, and when Shoshan shared the story of her resurrection and the truth of Jesus's claims, the woman turned her out.

Marcus's house was at the end, a home so grand that it had claimed the width of three houses. Each stone in the road was carefully, tightly fitted so neither man nor animal would trip. Every torch burned bright, the oil filled to the brim to give light until dawn. Insects flitted around the torches. Every home had multiple torches burning, and she wondered if anyone here had believed the stories of people rising from the dead. The torches were here for security, to protect the homes, not to welcome a stranger.

Everywhere she looked, she caught glimpses of a different world, of lives surrounded by artistry and seclusion. Coverings gave privacy to every window, and carved furniture peeked over every rooftop. What must it be like to be so rich?

Walking to the end of the street, Shoshan strained to see the iron scrollwork on the gate of Marcus's house, wanting to be sure this was indeed the right home. She traced the pattern with her finger then realized why it was hard to detect the pattern.

No torches burned outside his house.

Glancing around, Shoshan made sure no one was watching, then reached up to touch one of the torches that stood anchored on either side of the gate. The metal brackets that anchored each torch were cold. She retracted her hand, thinking. The torches had not burned for hours, maybe longer. A servant had let them go out. Marcus would have him whipped for this!

Tilting her head to one side, she listened. Marcus loved to entertain, especially when the wealthy of Rome were in town. Since Passover had ended, Romans guests were happily returning and reclaiming the streets. They did not like staying in Jerusalem when the Jews flooded the city from the surrounding villages.

The only sound coming from the house was a raven's caw, its harsh cry echoing over the darkness of the courtyard beneath. Squinting, Shoshan spied it sitting on the tile roof, like a lone herald announcing her arrival. No one answered, not even another bird.

A cloud rolled over the moon, deepening the shadows around her. Her heart beat harder, making her chest burn. This was not right. Where were the servants? The musicians, the singers, and cooks? This house always had activity and noise. Tonight, seeing the bare bones of the house shrouded in darkness, it looked more like a tomb than a home.

The insects keened louder as a stale, sour odor floated to her, making her recoil. The house, cloaked in shadows, seemed to be crouching, hoarding a terrible secret. Shoshan's legs felt weak, and her skin cold. Closing her eyes, she whispered His name for strength. *Jesus.*

He had walked out of His grave and then called her out of her own. What did she have to be afraid of? Death was not a threat to her, not anymore. Was there anything to fear if she did not fear death? Yes, her body seemed to say. There were many things to be afraid of.

Looking up and down the narrow street, she could see lights in the neighbor's upstairs windows. People were home and getting ready for bed. She was tempted to call out and ask for help, but she couldn't risk someone recognizing her. If anything had happened to Marcus or his wife, would they even know?

In this part of town, people were not as free to wander in and out of one another's houses. They were more formal. She shook herself then stiffened her back. It was entirely possible that her brother had left on a long voyage. Her mind fought the idea, of course, because no wealthy man would leave his house dark and unguarded. But she held on to the tiny hope, if only because she was afraid of what she would find behind the gates.

A servant from another house stepped outside a door and emptied a wash jar. The noise startled Shoshan, and she darted back into the shadows. The girl frowned, peering into the shadows in Shoshan's direction. *Enough*. Shoshan stepped into the light, raising a hand in greeting. She lifted her chin, trying to act like she belonged there, and put a hand on the iron gate.

The girl nodded, satisfied, and walked back inside. Breathing in relief that the girl had chosen not to scream, Shoshan forced her shaking hands to push against the iron gate. The hinges whined, and the gate slid open. Not a soul protested as she entered the courtyard. Above her, the raven flew off, its wings silent, its body silhouetted against the moon.

She entered the open-air garden, and the memories flooded back.

Marcus was so proud of this home. He'd designed everything himself, even the massive tile mosaic at her feet. In the daylight, the courtyard was a wash of color. The mosaic was made of thousands of tiny stones, each a different color, and the effect was like a portrait of his wife, Tullia. Antonius might even have cut the stones used for this painstaking artistry; only a very skilled craftsman could make these perfect, tiny squares.

Surrounding Tullia's beaming visage was a frame of blues and greens. Beyond that, everywhere Shoshan looked, greenery and blooms cascaded from tile retaining walls and clay pots. Marcus had a full-time gardener on staff to oversee the gardens, in addition to the house manager. Several of the more delicate blooming plants, however, had dropped their petals and hung limp, in dire need of water. Why had they been neglected?

To her right, Shoshan heard the gentle lap of water. Just past the two columns that stood silent guard was another portico and a pool. She remembered refreshing afternoons there. Against the far wall in that portico, a staircase led to lower rooms for entertaining guests.

A moth flitted past, startling her. The silence was unnatural. This was not a house that had ever known quiet or rest. It had been designed to impress and entertain, but now, all was dark and quiet. When had she last talked to Marcus?

Her mouth felt dry. Her eyes slowly adjusted to the limited moonlight. In the distance, the raven called. To the far right stood the staircase leading to the upper rooms, including the bedrooms. Above those was the roof for viewing the gardens and enjoying cool breezes. Craning her neck, she could not see anyone there.

A rock skidded across the garden path in front of her. Goose bumps prickled along her arms. She wasn't alone.

In the shadows near the main staircase, a man's figure stood, his eyes watching her. She froze. Then the man rushed at her. She yelped, jumping out of his way before she realized his arms were full. He was stealing. In his arms, he held household goods of all kinds. He carried mirrors, serving bowls, pearl-inlaid hairbrushes, the strangest assortment of things, all piled into a large acacia-wood serving bowl. He rushed past her, and an earring fell from his belt purse, landing at her feet on the pebble path. *Looter!*

She bent to pick it up, stunned, as he disappeared out the gate and into the street. His face, though, had seemed familiar. Where had she seen him before? Turning to look again, she saw him pause to glance in either direction before running. His footsteps grew faint, and then the night swallowed them up.

Marcus had been robbed!

But where was he? Where were Tullia and all the servants? She started to shout for help but then stopped, pushing her fist against her lips to force herself to remain quiet. She couldn't risk getting caught, especially in these circumstances.

The guards here might not know she was one of the resurrected ones being hunted in the northern part of the city, but they would look at her inexpensive clothes and know immediately she did not belong in this neighborhood. They would arrest her for the theft. It was an easy victory for them, an outsider brought to justice and a wealthy patrician's house defended. She'd be executed before her brother even returned home. And if her brother returned to find her standing in his home just after it had been robbed, who would he blame?

Her predicament horrified her. This was a trap.

CHAPTER ELEVEN

As Shoshan moved toward the gate, a sound from an upstairs window caught her attention. Pausing, she listened and waited. Again, she heard it. A muted noise, almost like a man's voice. It sounded like he was moaning, but so faint she might have imagined it. There were no lights. There was no movement.

Was there a man up there? Maybe the robbers had fought and hurt one of their own, leaving him behind to die. Or it could be an animal, she reasoned. Marcus might have had a guard dog, and the looters wounded it.

She looked around, but there was no oil lamp nearby and no way to light one even if there was. The darkness overwhelmed her, and she had no source of illumination other than the moon. Once she got inside those upstairs rooms, there would be no light at all except what came through the windows, and that would be minimal.

Dare she go and look? If she was alone in an upstairs room with a mortally wounded criminal, it would not end well.

But Jesus sent her here. He knew everything, didn't He, even her thoughts? Surely He knew what was waiting for her. He would not send her here without His reasons. Did she trust Him? Yes. But she also knew what she was seeing and hearing, and it terrified her.

Should she do what He asked? She looked down at her hands. He had raised her from the grave. No matter what happened up in those rooms, He held her life in His hands. No man could take that away from her or Him.

She walked to the far-right staircase and climbed. She guessed that the sound came from the bedrooms, because that was where Marcus's wife stored her jewelry. The thief had left with her earrings, so she knew that at least some jewelry had been stolen.

Upstairs, she stood outside a closed wooden bedroom door. She put her hand, still shaking, on the door and pushed. The door opened quietly, and moonlight flooded the room from the doorway.

A horrid, damp stench assaulted her nose, and she stepped back, waving a hand over her face. The room smelled of sweat and vomit.

A wheezing breath from the bed made her body feel cold. Someone was there, and they seemed to be dying. Or near death. She forced herself to the bed and peered down.

Covering her mouth to keep from screaming, she looked into Marcus's sunken eyes, his withered face. In the bed across from him, in the fetal position, her skin wet with droplets of perspiration, lay his wife, Tullia.

"Marcus!" Shoshan cried out, and flung the coverlet back, checking for injuries. "What did they do to you?" Had the thieves beaten him and his wife? Tortured them? She saw no marks of torture and no ropes binding their hands or feet.

Frowning, she saw the fear in Marcus's face as he stared up at her. He was terrified.

"How long have you been held captive?" she asked. Marcus tried to speak, but his voice was a low rasp. He raised a trembling hand to her, and she bent closer to hear. To her dismay, he pushed against her, trying to shove her back. His touch was as light as a child's. He wanted her to go? Why was he so afraid?

"They are gone," she said. "If you are worried about the thieves, they are gone."

His eyes remained wide with terror. His lips were pale and cracked at the corners. Tullia's eyes remained closed. Was she even alive? Shoshan was scared to check.

She turned to the bedside table, expecting to find cups and a jar for water, but there was nothing.

"It is all right," she murmured, trying to stay calm for his sake. "I will get water downstairs and bring it up. You will be safe until I return."

She forced herself to look closely at Tullia now. She looked in worse condition than Marcus, if that was possible. Her cheeks were hollow, her eyes sunken, and as she lay still, curled into a ball, her chest barely moved. She breathed but just barely. She still wore her robe over her tunic, as if she had collapsed into bed fully dressed and no one had helped her undress. Maybe no one had dared come near her. And there was another complication, one that made Shoshan's stomach flood with fear. Tullia's abdomen was swollen, in contrast to her thin arms and legs. Shoshan reached a hand toward her belly.

Marcus wheezed in terror and tried to lift a hand to stop her.

"What is it?" Shoshan whipped around to ask him. "What are you trying to tell me?" He couldn't be scared of her, could he? Since they'd had no contact, he could not have heard of her death. And she had assumed she could explain her resurrection when the time was right.

From bitter experience, she knew the story offended or frightened those who did not believe Jesus's claims of being the Son of God.

"Get out." Marcus sank back onto the bed, collapsing in exhaustion from speaking.

"Marcus, is Tullia pregnant?"

He had no more strength to reply. Shoshan turned back around and pressed her hand to Tullia's belly, ignoring a groan from Marcus.

A child moved within. Tullia was pregnant and probably near term.

Jesus, help me! Help her! Shoshan realized she was praying, but how odd to pray to Jesus. Jesus was not in heaven but on Earth. Her mind was muddled with too much. She couldn't make sense of anything.

She ran out the door and flew down the stairs, thankful she had been here a handful of times before the relationship soured for good. The layout of the house was still familiar to her. There was a well in the courtyard. Mercifully, she found wooden cups in the servants' rooms. Most everything else, though, was gone. The thieves had cleaned them out, taking everything of value and even things of very little value.

Marcus and Tullia were dying, and thieves had looted their house, leaving them to die.

No, this was not the work of thieves. She had recognized the man carrying the stolen goods. He had been their household manager. The thought made her stomach turn. Their own servants had looted their house, knowing Marcus and Tullia were dying.

She moved nimbly back up the stairs, careful not to spill the little ceramic jug of water, hoping the chips in the handle and rim didn't mean that it was going to shatter easily. Marcus and Tullia needed every drop to live. She poured the water into a wooden cup and moved toward Marcus. But she stopped. Although they'd been estranged for nearly three years, she knew him. He loved Tullia more than his own life. It was the sole reason Shoshan had never been able to hate him, even after he had disowned her as his sister. Marcus was capable of great love, even if he would never love her again.

Shoshan pressed the back of her hand to Tullia's forehead. Heat radiated off the poor woman. Lifting Tullia's head gently, she pressed the wooden cup to her lips and tipped it back. Tullia sputtered as the water dribbled into her mouth. Shoshan watched, holding her breath, as Tullia swallowed then opened her lips for more. Shoshan tipped the cup again and repeated her slow pouring until Tullia drained the last of the water.

Shoshan laid Tullia's head back on her pillow then pressed a hand to her huge abdomen. The baby kicked. Shoshan gasped in relief. A sudden wave of grief slammed against her heart, thinking of her own daughter. Not all babies survived, but Tullia's child had a chance. Maybe this was why Jesus gave her a second chance at life? To save Tullia's child?

Marcus moaned.

"The baby lives," Shoshan said over her shoulder. She refilled the cup and propped Tullia up again. After a little sip, Tullia sputtered and coughed, her eyes fluttering. Shoshan tipped the cup farther, encouraging Tullia to empty it. Her eyes opened, and she grabbed the cup as if she was desperate, choking and gulping at once, her eyes wild. Shoshan quickly refilled the water, and Tullia drained it again before collapsing back onto the pillows, her chest heaving with bigger breaths now.

Shoshan refilled the cup again and pressed it against Marcus's lips, but his eyes remained focused on his wife. He looked torn between distress and relief. He kept his lips firmly closed.

"Let her catch her breath. She has had enough for now," Shoshan whispered. "It is your turn to drink." Without waiting for an answer, she pressed the cup against his lips and tipped it back. At the first hint of water cascading over his mouth, Marcus opened his mouth and gulped. He was just as thirsty as his wife, and Shoshan had to go downstairs twice more for more water.

Marcus and Tullia fell into a long, fitful sleep after that. What were they suffering from? There were many possibilities, weren't there? No, only one disease could do this. But that disease was a death sentence in every way.

Shoshan sat with her back against the wall, watching over them, praying she was wrong, waiting for the dawn. She didn't know if thieves would return, and she had nothing to defend herself with. If her suspicions were correct, the servants would never dare return, not even if they remembered something left behind.

All she could do was pray. She had never had so much to pray for. How many times had she heard the old women in the market wishing they could have a second chance and start their lives over? If they could see her now! A cheating husband, a betraying best friend, a dying brother, a sister-in-law in danger of losing her child, thieves ransacking the house in the night, Roman guards hunting her in the daylight…

If Jesus was going to give her a new life, why had He not given her one with a smooth road?

The sun hit Shoshan's cheek, warming her face. The wood floor was gritty, and dust swirled in the air as she blinked open her eyes. Sitting up, she felt how dry her mouth was, and her muscles protested each movement. Her entire body was stiff and sore. She must have traveled miles by foot over the last twenty-four hours, barely eating or drinking. Sleeping on a wood floor hadn't helped.

She looked at the beds across the room. Marcus and Tullia were there, their chests rising and falling. They were alive, at least. And no one had broken in last night.

Shoshan's stomach growled. She needed to find food for them, as well as herself. She hadn't seen any in the kitchen the evening before when she fetched the water. How would she pay for it, though? Last night, she'd gotten the impression that the servants had robbed Marcus of everything he owned. Only the wooden serving pieces the servants used, which held little street value, were left, except for the ceramic jug with the chipped handle and rim. Shoshan had no hope of selling them to raise cash.

That was her first problem, then—how to buy food. The second problem was that buying food meant she had to go out in public in the daytime. If she got arrested, it wouldn't just mean she would die. It meant she would die, and so would Marcus and Tullia.

Shoshan had a terrible suspicion now that she was right about what they suffered from. Maybe the final truth had come to her in her dreams, or maybe it had taken the exhaustion of the night to clear away all other thoughts before she could finally accept it.

The Roman plague was in this house.

No wonder the servants had fled. Shoshan shot a nervous glance toward the bedroom door. Had they told anyone? If they did, Roman authorities would be at the gates downstairs soon enough. The Romans would declare a quarantine over the house. No one would be allowed in or out, for fear of spreading the disease across the city. It killed so many people and had so few remedies. None, actually, although the Romans tried magic and sorcery to combat it.

If anyone found out, Marcus and Tullia would die. Shoshan might survive but only if the Romans were kind enough to allow food to be dropped over the gates. She'd seen enough crucifixions to know not to put her hope in their kindness. Marcus had no money for bribes either. Not anymore. Anger burned in her heart as she thought of all the men Marcus had paid off in secret for the little luxuries in this city. Now, she knew, none would come to his aid. That sort of kindness was quickly forgotten when the plague was in a house.

If I stay, will I get the plague? She did not know. Virtually nothing was known about how the plague spread.

She stood and gave more water to both Marcus and Tullia. Both had perspired during the night. That was good. Shoshan ran her hand underneath their thighs. Neither had wet the bedding, though. That was not good, not at all. They needed more water throughout the day, and food.

Squaring her shoulders, she decided to brave the market in a few hours, when it was busiest. In a crowd there was less risk of being spotted. It would all work out. It had to. First, though, she had to find something downstairs to trade. Hopefully the servants had overlooked at least one thing she could use to barter at the market.

CHAPTER TWELVE

By midmorning, Tullia's fever had broken. She was sleeping deeply, each breath lifting her petite ribcage like a soft flutter. She looked so peaceful. Shoshan winced at her sister-in-law's serene beauty, so calm and undisturbed. The truth was sinister. This disease was a tricky enemy that could not be trusted. A fever that broke was not a good sign, not a promise that the worst was over. The fever almost always returned in the afternoon, and it could kill. Even if Tullia's fever had broken, it meant nothing. Shoshan had no way of knowing if the disease was getting better or worse. It was one of the reasons everyone feared this plague.

Shoshan left her and went downstairs again to continue looking through the kitchen and the servants' quarters. As she worked, her mind searched for memories of this disease. How had others treated it? She'd never paid much attention before. Why would she? This plague was a scourge known to the Romans, not those in Jerusalem. Sometimes if an official or wealthy merchant traveled outside Israel, they came home with the disease. Their houses would be quarantined if they had not died before it was discovered. Often, they were dead within days though. Pregnant women had a dreadful time with it. They miscarried their children before dying themselves. It was a frightening and barbaric illness.

But it afflicted those in Rome much more often than anyone here. Shoshan spent her childhood in Rome, but she recalled very little about the disease. Why would she? Children didn't pay close attention to diseases and remedies. She only remembered basic facts, including that the Romans said it was caused by bad air. They were careful to avoid travel in areas of stagnant water where the stench of decay was strong. But Jerusalem had no swamps and no areas of stagnant water. How had Marcus and Tullia contracted it? She would have to solve that mystery later. They must have traveled somewhere, but the house showed no signs of a recent trip. But of course, the servants would have stolen any purchases or cargo.

Right now, she had to figure out how to treat it. Would anyone in the market here know of a cure? Surely knowledge had increased in recent years. When she was a child living in Rome, she had seen a few victims. But they had been dead already and on the way to their graves.

She remembered one victim more than the others. It was a young girl, no more than three years old, her body carried on a tiny stretcher between two men. Behind them, a donkey pulled a cart of large rocks. She remembered the moment vividly.

"What are the rocks for?" Shoshan had grabbed her mother's robe and yanked it closer.

Mother rested a hand on her shoulder. "They will place the rocks over the body. The rocks will stop the demon from escaping and making the rest of the family ill."

A wave of terror swept over her, thinking of all those heavy, sharp rocks placed over that tiny, fragile body. How was it possible that a demon had entered a little girl? And why would rocks stop a demon from going where it pleased?

She had wanted to ask more questions, but Mother had pulled her inside and set her to work. They were going to bring a meal to the bereaved family, even if the family was Roman, not Jewish.

Leaving the memory, Shoshan now worked her way through the kitchen, searching for something to barter with at the market. There was nothing. Last night, when she had found the wooden cups and broken jug, was that really all those wicked servants left behind? It seemed impossible they had stolen everything from a house like this, but it was clear they had. It must have taken them hours, maybe even days, to loot the estate. Meanwhile, knowing Marcus and Tullia were suffering, the servants hadn't even called for a doctor. If they had, a doctor would have visited by now, bringing whatever medicines he had. But the house would have been locked down and under guard when she arrived. Marcus and Tullia would be under a death sentence. This disease had so little mercy, even less than Rome.

The image of the little girl's body, and all those rocks, flashed through her mind again. Panic struck like a flash of pain under her ribs. She had to do something.

Without warning, exhaustion flooded her mind and body. It was all too much for her, and her body seemed frail, too delicately made for the conditions of this harsh life. Murder, betrayal, disease, terror? Where could she get the strength to live? But she had, once, even before she met Jesus. Now that she knew Him, and He had raised her, surely He would give her another source of strength. There was not enough human strength to live in this human world. Jesus had to offer another source of strength if she was going to survive.

She lowered herself, nearly collapsing, beside the courtyard pool to sit. The pool water, usually pristine and inviting, was dotted with leaves from the gardens. She tried to think. How long had her brother been in bed, unable to oversee the home? A soft trickle from the fountain in the center was the only noise in the house. Each drop caused tiny ripples to run across the top of the pool, sending the leaves bobbing on the surface. If Marcus had not appeared outside the gates for weeks, someone should be suspicious by now.

Outside the gates, she could hear the neighbors going about their day, with no idea of the drama playing out behind these walls. People in the street spoke in plain, loud voices, donkeys brayed, carrying loads through the street, their hooves clopping with a steady rhythm. She had to get up. The market would be bustling.

But first, she had to make a plan and think of what she needed to buy, then work quickly to get off the streets and back home before anyone recognized her. Where should she go in the market? They needed food, but they also needed medicine. She just had no idea what kind of medicine, or who to ask. It also had to be done without revealing why she needed it.

Since her childhood in Rome, the doctors must have found solutions to treat the disease. With so many Romans living in Jerusalem, the physicians here would have that knowledge. Shoshan could be discreet. She would find someone, a Roman citizen perhaps, who knew how to treat the disease according to the newest ways of medicine. There was nothing the Romans couldn't do when they chose to.

And she needed to buy the right food at the market. Marcus and Tullia were so thin and weak. There was no way to tell how long it had been since the servants last fed them, so giving them solid food might not work. They were also badly dehydrated when Shoshan arrived. It had been good to give them water, since water might have been all they could take. A broth, then, was what she needed. If she could find some meat, hopefully on the bone, and prepare a broth, it would strengthen them until they could take solid food.

And what about a doctor? Shoshan had never used a Roman physician and didn't know how to hire one. Marcus was close to the Sadducees only because he loved the status, but he had no close relationships with rabbis. Still, Shoshan could go to his synagogue and plead for mercy, asking them to send a Hebrew healer, but how could she do that without revealing her identity and Marcus's plight? Every solution only led to the same dead end. No one could discover her identity or the presence of the plague.

The only thing working in her favor was that Antonius had no idea where she was and would never think to look for her here. He knew Marcus had disowned her and that if she turned up on her brother's doorstep, she would be thrown out immediately.

Shoshan laughed and drew her robe tighter around her, trying to work up the courage to stand and go. She had to go to the market with no money, plus evade the Roman guards, especially the one called Clemens. It was impossible, probably, but Jesus had done the impossible. She had to believe He could do it again.

At least she could assume Antonius would not be in this part of the city, or the market, since laborers did not mix with the elite classes. She wondered what Antonius would do if he caught her in public. Calling for the guards was the obvious answer, but he had killed her once, she was sure of that. He might not wait for the guards if he saw an opportunity to do it once more.

Besides, he was probably more concerned with finding Miriam, and Shoshan was looking for Jesus. He was known to travel in and out of Jerusalem, wandering the countryside. There was a chance Antonius was already out of the city. That should have relieved her fears, but it hurt. He wanted Miriam, not her.

Shoshan had a new life, but the wounds of her old one still burned. She hadn't done anything to deserve the betrayal of Miriam and Antonius. Didn't that mean, somehow, that there would be an extra measure of grace from God to survive it?

A rasp of breath from Tullia in the bedroom above made her shudder. Tullia hadn't done anything to deserve that disease. Where was her grace for this moment?

Maybe I am the measure of grace for her, sent by God. Here I am, worrying about my life, when I need to be moving fast.

Shoshan carefully moved through the servants' living quarters one last time. Desperate, she looked in every possible hiding spot but found nothing of value. Even the linens had been stripped from the servants' beds. A cobweb hung in a corner of the bedroom off the kitchen.

With no money and nothing to trade, how could she get what she needed at market? She couldn't risk stealing. Marcus said she had a guilty face, that everything she felt showed on it. People would already be curious about her, a stranger at their market, and watch her more closely. Although she was wearing Miriam's expensive clothes, they were brightly colored because Miriam loved the attention. Any hope of blending in might be misplaced.

Marcus should be the one in charge now, not her. He always had a plan. Having grown up in Rome, he was good at finding things in the streets, straps dropped by soldiers, tassels fallen from horse's tack. He sold his treasures at the market for a nice profit, hoarding his money in a loose brick in the wall behind his bed.

Little Shoshan had secretly watched him at night when he thought everyone was asleep. He would pull the brick out, tuck a coin in, and replace the brick. She had watched with fascination, and a gnawing dread, as the moonlight glinted off the ever-growing pile of coins in his stash. He was a boy of secrets. The secrets were living things that grew inside him like a garden, one that he kept walled off from her. She was afraid of what grew there, behind the walls of his heart.

A thought shocked her with its absolute clarity.

Standing, she padded softly upstairs, relieved to find him asleep, a sheen of sweat on his brow. Leaning over the head of the bed, she pressed a palm against the stone wall, running her hand over the stones until she found it.

One stone was not mortared tightly against the others. It wiggled side to side when she pushed it. Bits of dust trickled down as she angled it back and forth and finally pulled it free.

Her brother's eyes fluttered open.

She held one finger to her lips.

"Do not wake Tullia," she urged.

He grabbed her arm tightly. His strength surprised her.

"You are dead," he said, his voice hoarse. He must have heard of her death. The thought chilled her. What connection did he still maintain with Antonius?

"I was," she replied, setting the brick on the floor. There was no time to consider the implications of his statement. Suddenly, she had all the money she needed, and the market was open. Tullia would receive the food and medicine she needed.

Inside the cavity was a stack of coins. Coin by coin, she plucked out the money and filled the bag on her waist. Marcus's eyes followed her every move.

"You will be flogged for this," he whispered, a sheen of sweat appearing on his brow.

Stopping, she rested a hand on his arm. He flinched at her touch. He must be thinking she too was only here to rob him. He was half delirious from the fever.

"I will explain everything when I get back," she said. "I am trying to save Tullia and you, but I need money to go to the market. I promise that I will come back."

Next, she took off her robe and draped it over the foot of Tullia's bed. She carefully lifted Tullia and removed the robe she was wearing, leaving her only in a thin tunic. The servants hadn't taken the robe, probably in fear of contracting the plague. Shoshan was exposed to it already, so taking her robe would not matter. She tucked the bed linens around Tullia's shoulders, then left before Marcus could question her. If she explained everything to him now, the shock might kill him. He could not possibly understand how desperate his situation was, or how near death his wife and unborn child were.

And he certainly would not be able to handle the other truth, that Shoshan had been lying dead in the grave only a few days ago, and now she was his only hope of saving his family. With just a short while until the Sabbath began, she had to hurry. Once the markets closed, they would not reopen for twenty-four hours. Marcus and Tullia, especially Tullia, might not survive that long without proper food.

Walking down the stairs, coins in hand, she heard the noise before her brain registered what it meant to her plans.

A steady clatter all around and a crack of thunder in the distance. A rainstorm had begun. Her stomach felt cold and hard. There would be no market. Not until the rain stopped.

But she needed food, and medicine, and a physician's counsel! *Stop the rain, Lord!*

The rain continued throughout the day and into the night. Shoshan sat in the stairwell, coins in hand, eyes dazed in painful disbelief. At last, she stood and did the only thing she could. She brought water to Tullia and Marcus. He watched her with blazing eyes, and she tried to explain why she had taken his money and returned to the room empty-handed. Hour by hour, Tullia grew weaker.

When the shofar blew, Shoshan pressed her hands over her mouth to keep from crying out. The temple priests blew the shofar in the late afternoon to alert the city that Sabbath was approaching. They had to finish their business and close shop, and foreigners preferred to leave until after the gates reopened. When the sun set tonight, all the shops would be closed for twenty-four hours. The market would be closed too. There would be no way to get food or medicine, not without a miracle.

The rain droned on.

CHAPTER THIRTEEN

Early on the first day after Sabbath, Shoshan debated while she paced in the courtyard, listening for the sounds of the street. She would be first at market and did not care if the vendors took advantage of her eagerness to buy.

Sabbath had passed without any answer from the Lord, or any reprieve from the rain. With only water, cup by cup, she had given drink to Marcus and Tullia, bathed their fevered brows, and moistened their cracked lips. Her legs ached from the numerous trips up and down the stairs to fetch more water. It had not seemed like enough in the face of this plague.

But it had been. Perhaps that was a miracle, after all.

She hurried downstairs and turned to close the gate, and her breath stopped, alarm seizing her again. Footprints in the mud caught her eye as she secured the gates. The prints were made by a man wearing boots, judging by the shape and size. But the depth of them scared her more. They were sunk into the mud, as if the man had stood in the rain for a long time in one spot. He had stood at the gate, staring into the courtyard.

She followed the steps around the house and found another deep-set pair. Placing her feet inside, ignoring the mud that clung to the hem of her robe, she looked up. Whoever had stood here in the rain last night had stared toward the bedroom where Marcus and Tullia were. Where last night Shoshan had been caring for them.

A man had been here in the night, watching and waiting. For what? She mentally ticked off the most likely choices. A thief, returning for more plunder. Antonius, the murderer, come to finish her off in secret. Or a Roman guard named Clemens who, somehow, got word she was hiding here and wanted to arrest her. His career would be secured by her arrest and death. Shoshan put one hand over the bag at her belt, pressing the coins tightly to her waist. Ducking her head, she avoided meeting anyone's eye and hurried to market.

Anyone could be watching.

The market at this end of the city was smaller but more refined. The first few stalls held fat dark figs that glistened next to wood bowls overflowing with dried flax and wheat, finely milled. At the slightest breeze, such as a sudden turn of a customer and the whip of their sleeve, a thin whisp would fly up and away from the bowl. Never had Shoshan seen grains so finely milled—they were light as a cloud. She was used to eating grains as thick as sand, with the occasional pebble.

She purchased a bag of each grain to make bread. Maybe that would be easy for Tullia to digest. When the merchant told her the final cost, Shoshan felt sick. She'd brought money for shopping based on her purchases at her market, not this one. And there was more to buy.

Tullia needed strength, and for that, Shoshan needed meat. Medicine might be too much to hope for now. Her funds were low.

As she walked farther into the stalls, she passed a table of linens. The linens were outrageously expensive. She had to resist the urge to touch a robe that was spilled across the table like it was woven of water.

Shoshan had forgotten what luxury Marcus was accustomed to. She continued on, hoping she did not look as lost as she felt. When she reached the end of the market, the sunlight burned her eyes. Blinking, she stood with the bags of grain in one hand, her other hand clutching her belt to her waist.

Where Marcus's servants bought their meat, she did not know. She couldn't risk going to her own market or butcher, however, and she didn't want to go to the Fish Gate. Tullia needed meat, not fish. Biting her lip, she thought. Where to go next? Who bought and sold without asking too many questions?

People in all sorts of precarious situations needed the same things she did. The downtrodden and forgotten had always been hidden away in the city. It made it easier to avoid them, but now she needed their expertise if she was going to survive in the shadows.

Jesus, I wish You were here with me now. Is it all right if I go to them for help? They are unclean. But I cannot think of any other solution.

She set out down the street that led toward the back of Herod's Theater. With every step, she felt a catch in her breath, waiting for God to stop her. Nothing happened. She just took step after step until at last she was in the other world, the world of the painted players and magicians, the acrobats and those born with rare and pitiful conditions. None were members of her synagogue, and therefore no one knew her identity.

Suddenly, she felt shame for that. They needed Jesus as much as she did.

A flurry of activity was occurring in little clusters, a market of their own thriving here. Many of the unfortunate ones were sellers, and she saw that other citizens of the city had come to buy from them. Some citizens were Romans, others were Jews. All were here because these people had goods that others did not.

Medicines and tinctures were sold by a woman wearing a thick Egyptian amulet. Looking around, Shoshan realized there was a great deal of magic and Roman and Greek gods for sale. The Romans loved magic.

But, as far as she could tell, there were no real physicians here. She didn't want to ask a sorceress or magician for help, especially not if it involved witchcraft, but surely someone knew of remedies she could try, things that had nothing to do with magic.

Off to the side of the secret market, she spied a bale of straw that served as a table, with a plain cloth draped over it. Clay jars, in the shape of figurines, sat on display for purchase. Each was no bigger than an apricot. Some had bodies of men, others of animals. She was familiar with these sorts of jars. Usually, the shape of the jar indicated how its contents were to be used. Each probably held small amounts of dried herbs or ointments, and none were used in magic or supernatural rituals.

An old man with a patch over one eye sat on a stool behind the table. His working eye was milk-colored, and she wondered how well he saw.

"What is this for?" Shoshan pointed to a jar in the shape of a man.

"Oh, that is for the swelling of the joints. When fingers turn painful and swollen." How had he seen what she pointed to? She leaned side to side to see if his one good eye followed, but it did not.

Painful, swollen joints were not her problem. She bit her lip, looking around at the other vendors nearby.

He smiled and tipped his chin down. "I know why you are here," he said quietly.

"You do?" she replied, surprised and wary, maintaining her distance. He might be charming her or attempting a magic trick. She had no use for either.

He tapped the patch over his missing eye. "It sees far." He laughed lightly at his joke, but she wondered if it was a joke at all.

She swallowed, although her mouth was dry as bone. She refused to reply or participate until she knew his intention.

"You seek help for your brother and his wife," he whispered.

How did he know that? She could barely hear him, but that was what he said, she was certain. Folding her arms, she felt her heart pounding beneath her tunic. Who else knew why she was here?

"Why do you look so skeptical?" he asked.

She moved closer and lowered her face so no one could overhear. "Who told you about my brother? How do you know who I am?"

"I know you are a follower of Jesus." Worry lines burrowed across his forehead. At the mention of that name, anyone on the street was in danger. He was done teasing and laughing now. The man peered into her face with his one clear, good eye.

"How do you—" She had to stop herself because he was already answering.

"A few of your kind have come through the market. Resurrected ones. You all look the same, every one of you, with that dazed expression as you look around at the world. It is as if you are seeing it for the first time. I would like to think I understand."

He tapped his patch over the missing eye again. "Look at me. I appear to be the same man I was before I met Jesus. But He changed me completely. What I see now is far more valuable. That is what Jesus understood about me, even before I could put it into words. You understand?"

Shoshan made a noise, a little start of a word, then swallowed. She didn't understand anything, not about this man or about his eyes.

"What do you see, exactly?" she finally managed. "How did you know why I am here?"

He leaned back, beaming with joy. *He must know Jesus*, Shoshan thought. Only Jesus could leave someone so content, even if their life was filled with hardships.

"The only answer to both questions is Jesus. When I met Jesus, I had a hard heart. That is what needed healing, not my eyes. Now I can see what matters. I see people in need," the man said. "They are everywhere! Why did I never know that before? But when I saw you, something whispered in my heart. I just knew."

He sat up suddenly and took a deep breath, releasing it. "When you give Jesus your life, everything is different, even if it looks the same."

Shoshan's mind felt like it was being pressed between two enormous stones. God had helped this man to see her distress, but he sold wares among the unclean. Why hadn't God moved him to another area of the city, to live among believers or the faithful members of the synagogue?

Maybe the people in desperate need of help came through here. Maybe they were afraid to go to the synagogues, especially after Jesus's execution.

She had so many questions and so much confusion, but the only thing that mattered now was Marcus and Tullia.

"Have you treated anyone with fever?" she asked. Lowering her voice, she leaned closer, closing the distance he created when he leaned back. "The Roman plague?"

The old man opened his mouth to reply, but he was interrupted.

"What kind of fever?" a woman standing nearby asked, squinting in curiosity. Thankfully, she hadn't heard the second part of Shoshan's question.

"A fever that comes and goes," Shoshan replied. That was truthful. The fever was better midmorning, she had noticed, then returned with a vengeance in late afternoon.

"Be gone." The woman made a sweeping motion with her hands, as if judging the robes she wore and dismissing her concern. "A servant like you in a noble house? Your master can bring a physician."

Shoshan looked down, shocked, then remembered she was wearing Tullia's robe.

The old man looked as if he wanted to cut her off from saying anything else, but she couldn't leave this woman with any hints about her real predicament.

"You know how the ruling class are. He is too busy with his own troubles," Shoshan said quickly. "This is my task. I have to succeed or face punishment." It was all true, in its way.

"Have you got money?" The woman pressed her lips into a thin line.

"Yes!" Shoshan replied.

"Then, bird claw is what I use. Burn them during the midnight ritual to keep the fever away." The woman pointed to a bowl of dark nail clippings near her feet.

Shoshan blanched and averted her eyes.

"But they are expensive, so you will pay me well."

"Do you have anything else?" Shoshan asked. "I do not use magic." She could tell the woman was doubly offended now. "My master does not approve." That was not a lie, not exactly.

"Who said anything about magic?" the woman snapped. "It is medicine. Everyone knows how powerful the smoke from a burning claw is."

Finished with Shoshan, she turned to attend to other customers.

A boy, about twelve or thirteen, stepped toward her. His face was scrubbed clean, but his clothes were patched and dirty. His tunic looked too short for him. He had grown out of it, she thought.

"Fevers are controlled by the stars. The Dog Star is the worst offender." He spoke with absolute authority. Shoshan bit the inside of her cheek to keep from smiling. She didn't want to hurt his feelings or offend anyone else today.

"You must use medicine," he continued. "But whatever medicine you buy, use it when the Dog Star is bright."

"Thank you," she offered.

He waited, but she caught him sneaking glances at the old man, not her. Did they know each other?

She looked around, but he did not seem to have a mother nearby either, or anyone who would scold him for lecturing an adult. Stars, bird claws, midnight rituals? What she needed was Jesus. She'd seen the miracles He had performed. Where was He? Why didn't He help her now? Why lead her here, and give the old man a revelation but no practical advice? What was the point of it all?

As she stood debating where to go next, the boy began arguing the merits of the Dog Star with the woman selling the bird claws.

As he did, the old man frantically motioned for Shoshan to step closer. He reached beside his straw bale and produced a dried stalk of a plant with broad, clubbed leaves. "Boil this. The patient must drink it several times a day."

After slipping the plant into her bag, Shoshan offered a coin, but the man shook his head. "If anyone asks, you found it growing in the hills."

He held up one hand, and it shook, either with fear or age. "This is the only plant that seems to be effective against this disease. Do not waste your money on anything else. But be warned—if the Romans find out I helped you and did not report your situation to the city, we will both be dead before sunrise."

Shoshan hurried away.

"You do not want a bird's claw?" the boy called after her, his voice plaintive, cutting through the chatter and din of the market. "The Dog Star is almost at its peak!"

Make him go away, she prayed silently. The boy brought unwanted attention.

He followed her at a distance, calling out, offering to help her and guide her to other merchants. She'd seen street children like him before and knew his plan. If he brought a paying customer to a merchant's stall, he would get a coin or a meal, sometimes a place to sleep for the night. He didn't care about her.

Still, he was relentless in his pursuit. Even after she left the market, he followed from a distance, though he stopped yelling. She could not risk this boy following her all the way home, drawing attention to her, but what could she do?

God had refused another of her prayers, which made no sense. Or maybe He couldn't hear her praying over the shouts of this boy, she thought grimly. Either way, she had to finish her shopping and get home before any thieves returned to find the house unguarded. Or her murderer, Antonius, decided to visit. Or a Roman guard came looking for her.

She caught sight of the boy ducking behind a wall, trying to avoid being seen.

There could be spies everywhere.

CHAPTER FOURTEEN

Before she went home, she needed one more thing. Her final stop was to buy meat. But buying flour for bread and a small skin of goat's milk had cost more money than she expected. She opened the bag at her side and counted her coins. It was not enough to buy quality meat. Even buying a bone to boil would cost too much.

Her panic became a storm cloud, creeping closer with every passing minute. She had bought necessities, nothing more, and yet had run out of money. Of course, she could get more from Marcus's stash, but could she risk wandering the streets again? The market here had no obvious meat vendors. If she hadn't found a butcher in the market the first time, she might not succeed on her second try either. She couldn't risk an arrest just to wander around and hope she stumbled across what she needed.

And meat was the one ingredient she knew that Marcus and Tullia needed, truly needed, to rebuild their strength. Milk and bread soaked in milk would be good, but they weren't ready for other solid foods yet.

Why did everything have to be so hard if she was doing His will?

As she approached Marcus's home, she noticed that the streets had dried and the footprints in the mud that covered the stones were gone. The watcher, whoever he was, might come again tonight. If he was too scared to consider forcing his way inside...then he would have to be content to watch the home from a distance. What would instill a little fear? Perhaps if he thought everyone was home or new servants had been hired, he would be afraid, but she had no idea how to do that. She needed to buy a little time for herself, and that required cleverness, not money.

The torches...yes! The torches outside the gate were black with old soot and cold to the touch. They announced to everyone that the home was unguarded, because a vigilant servant would never leave the torches unlit.

Relieved that she had at least one tiny way to protect herself and the home, she set her purchases down inside the gates then went upstairs to bring Marcus and Tullia water. They were both breathing, praise to God. Tullia's eyes fluttered open briefly as Shoshan tipped the cup to her lips.

Courage stirred in Shoshan's heart, as if in response. The day had not been a total failure. She hadn't found meat, but she had medicine, plus flour and milk, and she would light the torches in a moment. It seemed like an important step.

Resting a hand on Tullia's abdomen, she concentrated, hoping for a sign. The baby did not move. Fear snuck back into her heart. But babies did not always move, did they? Shoshan tried to remember her own pregnancy, and returning to those memories was like peeling back the scab over a deep wound. Painfully, carefully, she pressed her eyes shut and remembered those days. The baby, her daughter, had not always moved. Her daughter had been most active...*when*? Shoshan squeezed her eyes tightly. *When*?

Just after I ate, yes. The cold, dead torches would have to wait. She hurried downstairs to begin work on a meatless broth. The baby needed food. A good broth, even if it was only herbs and a bit of flour, might make the difference between life and death. She refused to wonder which one of them she had a chance of saving. Tullia and her baby...Their fates were bound together and in her hands.

In the kitchen, she reached for a pot and then stared, dumbfounded. There was no pot. How could she have forgotten? The servants had stolen everything. Clenching her fists, she wanted to scream in frustration.

Jesus had sent her here. Why was everything going wrong?

Maybe she was the real problem, not her unanswered prayers. She seemed to be inept at everything, from shopping and budgeting to remembering what she needed. Maybe that was the reason Antonious betrayed her. She wanted to fall to the floor and weep with frustration and exhaustion, but there was no time for tears, not if she wanted Tullia and the baby to live. She had to keep moving and keep fighting.

How could she get a pot? If she tried to buy or borrow one, it might create suspicion, especially if anyone realized it was for Marcus's house. A stranger who needed to borrow a cooking pot for a wealthy man's estate would seem odd. Needing a moment to think, she walked outside the gates and grabbed one of the torches that had burned out. At least she could do that much, relight the torches.

Shoshan crossed the narrow street to the neighbor's property, where she tipped the torch to the one burning at their gate. As she turned slowly, balancing the heavy torch as it sputtered to life and dripped grease, she stopped in shock.

The beggar boy from the market outside the theater stood in the street, staring at her. His eyes twinkled with what looked like delight, as if he had won their game of hide-and-seek.

Her body went cold with fear. She looked behind him, expecting a guard or Antonius, the torch sputtering and flickering between them.

"What are you doing here?" she breathed.

"The old man said you would need help," the boy said, walking toward her. "I tried to ask you what I could help you with, but you just kept running away."

She stepped back, eyes sweeping the street all around. He was too little to be of any help. This might be a trick, and someone could be hiding, about to jump out and assault her, paid by Antonius. Or a servant who wanted access to the house again.

With a carefree whistle, he approached her. Standing before her, ignoring the torch she held out like a club she could use as a weapon, he looked up into her face. His eyes were wide and brown, and his face bright. He grinned, as if he did not notice her panic, and she noticed that some of his teeth were missing. He had probably lost them to disease or decay. Had no one looked after him?

"Who sent you?" she asked. Despite her fear, she wanted to know more. And she couldn't help it. She wanted to help him. No boy this age should live on the street.

"The old man at the market. I told you."

He reached for the torch. Although confused, she didn't resist him. His demeanor was not that of a sinister trickster or spy. He seemed like a truthful, earnest boy, and one who was all alone in the world. But she didn't know if there were still people in this world she could trust. Certainly not her best friend or the man she had pledged her entire being to. Clearly, she was not a good judge of people and their intentions.

Still, when he reached for the torch, she let him take it from her hand.

He held the torch carefully and, one by one, lit the torches outside Marcus's home. It was as if he automatically knew what to do. But they were the only unlit torches on the street, so maybe it was easy to guess what was needed.

She bit her lower lip, unsure. Trusting Antonius got her killed.

Trusting Me gave you life.

Shoshan whirled around, but He was nowhere to be seen. Shoshan rested her hand over her heart, where His voice had seemed to resonate. It was as if Jesus could speak directly to her heart now.

Without asking, the boy walked through the gate and lit a fire inside the courtyard. Shoshan followed, too shocked to argue. He lit another fire in the kitchen.

"Does your mother know you are here?" she asked when her voice returned.

"My mother is gone." He shrugged and returned the torch to its holder outside the gate. A second later, he stood in front of her again. "What now?"

"What do you mean?" she asked, still looking at him like he was speaking in another language. Was his mother dead, or had she abandoned him?

"What do I do now?" he asked.

She didn't need a boy to take care of, not when she was already taking care of Marcus and Tullia. Plus, he would be useless if a guard or Antonius attacked the home.

"Great houses like this"—he motioned around him—"have many servants. You have only me. What do I do first?"

He wants to be hired as a servant? She stared at him, still unsure what to do. He did not look like a Hebrew or a Roman. He was certainly not trained as a servant for a fine house—that would be impossible for a boy his age. Jobs were not easy to find, especially for a boy his age. He was a homeless beggar, and Marcus would never want a beggar off the streets working in his home.

Marcus would never have wanted a lot of things. Neither would she, she realized. But she might be a beggar herself now. She had no home or family anymore.

She reached into her belt and produced two coins. "I need a pot to cook a stew in. If anyone has a bone broth already made, bring that."

He turned abruptly and left.

She watched him leave, his posture stiff, his arms swinging at his sides. He was a boy, pretending to be an adult. She probably had just given away two coins, never to be seen again. If he was smart, he'd buy himself plenty of food and never return.

What was she doing, anyway? Marcus would never approve or agree to keep this boy in his home. The boy might have bad friends that followed him, not to mention hiring a child beggar would threaten Marcus's reputation in Roman society. But if Marcus wanted his unborn child to live, they all had to risk losing their lives as they knew them.

This was her second life, a life she had been given, but every decision felt like a choice to give it up again.

Shoshan leaned against the bedroom wall, peering out the window into the street below. To anyone passing by, it would look like Marcus was at home and all was normal. The torches burned, smells of dinner wafted from the kitchen, and now and then voices echoed from the stairwell. Shoshan, however, knew how wrong everything was behind the iron gates.

Drinking a cup of cold broth, her first of the day, she felt it hit her empty stomach like a shock. Her body woke with the sensation, eager for the energy a good meal would bring. She had kept vigil through the night again over Tullia and Marcus. Shoshan had removed the tunic she borrowed from Tullia, setting it near the bedroom doorway. When there was time, she'd wash it and the veil, making sure to return them to the chest in perfect condition. For today's work, her stained clothes would suffice.

The little street beggar who had followed her home was downstairs working. He had been successful in his errands last night, even bringing her back a coin. She had been shocked, but relieved, when he appeared at the gates bearing his purchases. Thanks to him, they now had a pot, though it was used and dented, and he had bought a jar of broth. Still, she wished she had bought meat when she was at market. The broth would be gone in a few hours.

She hadn't even discovered his real name yet. He went by a nickname, Haraka, which meant *fast*. It was fitting. He could talk his way into anything before she knew what he had done. But she had forbade him from showing his face to Marcus. She hadn't yet won her brother's trust. He still thought she might be a ghost. If he saw this boy, nothing but stick-thin bones and bravado, he would panic. That would probably kill Marcus, given how weak he was.

How she wished she could have Jesus with her, telling her what to do, assuring her that everything would be all right. Why had He raised her to life only to be surrounded by danger and death? This new life was no easier than her first. Not in circumstances, anyway.

"You were dead," Marcus said.

"You are awake." Shoshan turned. Going to his bedside, she pressed the back of her hand to his forehead. It was surprisingly cool, although his skin had a fine layer of grit. The fever that had made him sweat all night had left salt on his skin. She picked up a linen, soaked it in a bowl of fresh water. and washed his face as she talked.

"What do you remember?" she asked.

"You were dead," he repeated. He eyed her as if he was trying to figure out the con but could not guess what she might want.

She needed to tell him what had happened to him, to his house and servants. He needed to understand how desperate his situation was, but the truth of it might be too much. She grimaced inwardly, hating to put off the revelation any longer. Glancing at Tullia, who was still sleeping, she knew there was no good time to tell him, not when he was weak and unable to do anything. But if she waited for Tullia to be awake and listen, that would threaten her recovery too. The fastest way through this danger was to explain it all again, quickly, a short version. She'd tried once before, but Marcus had been in and out of his fevers.

"Yes," Shoshan replied finally. "You are right. I died. I woke in my grave, and Jesus told me to come here. When I did, I discovered you and Tullia like this." She omitted the part about his house being looted and the betrayal of his servants. And she omitted the part about her daughter. She could not tell him that. If he began to dwell on the fact that babies did not always survive their delivery, the terror would overwhelm him. She still wasn't sure she could handle nursing a pregnant woman whose life was in danger. But if Tullia and the baby survived, the pain of seeing a child born healthy and whole— that might break her heart all over again. Could she endure that?

"Dead people do not return," Marcus said. "And yet, here you are, and you claim you were dead. If you are not a ghost, what are you?" Marcus stared at her like she was a stain on a cobblestone. An unpleasant curiosity, nothing more.

"I did not fake my death, if that is what you are thinking," she quickly countered. "My death was real, whether you believe that or not. The funeral was real. I assume you were not there."

That hurt. *My daughter was real too,* she wanted to yell at him. But that was her burden right now.

He looked away, dismissing her. He had mastered the cold, unspoken commands of the upper class. Frustration rose up, and she gritted her teeth as she fought to remain calm. It was important that he believed her, because he had to understand the danger he was in. He had to know that she was his best hope for survival, as well as Tullia's.

"Marcus, I was dead. I was returned to life. I know that sounds extreme, or like a fireside story. I am not the only one who experienced it though. You have heard Jesus was crucified?"

He cut his eyes back to her and nodded, the slightest trace of disbelief in the smirk playing at the corner of his thin, tight lips.

Revulsion sprang up. He smirked at the image of Jesus experiencing such horror. Did he think Jesus deserved that? She turned away, composing herself. Clearing her throat, then coughing, it was as if her body tried to dislodge the fury and indignation that threatened to spill out. Too many cruel things had happened to her to be patient with Marcus, but that is exactly what was needed.

"Jesus rose from the grave," Shoshan continued, speaking evenly. "He rose first, then others came out too. None of us who were raised with Him understand why we were chosen or allowed to see this second life. But we are not like Him. We are ordinary. My body is the same. There is nothing special or new. But Jesus… He is risen in a new body. I have seen Him, Marcus, talked to Him, face-to-face, just as I am talking to you."

Marcus's eyes darted back and forth as if trying to visualize the story, and then finally came to rest on her face. His expression was flat, maybe from exhaustion or disbelief. That was too much to tell him at one time. Telling him the rest right now, about her daughter, or Antonius's crimes and Miriam's betrayal, would definitely be too much. Those stories, all her private griefs, she had to keep secret for Marcus's sake. She had readily accepted being raised from the dead, but that was only because she had had other shocks to grapple with. Antonius and Miriam, to begin with. Then finding Marcus and Tullia in this condition. She drew a deep breath. Her resurrection had been a wildly unexpected miracle, but she hadn't contemplated it yet. There had been no time.

"We can talk about all that later, when you are stronger, yes?" she said. "I will answer any question you have, but all of them can wait. Right now, I must find a way to get you both healthy. Can you tell me when you first fell ill?"

"Where are my servants?" Marcus's voice rasped, and his eyes darted from corner to corner of the room. The conversation was too much for him. He was growing weak, losing his senses. "You think I have not noticed? What have you done?"

This conversation was not what she wanted. "They were gone when I arrived."

"You probably think that if you kill me, you will inherit the estate," he replied. His face drained of color until it resembled the hue and texture of old papyrus. He needed more broth and water.

"I do not want your money," she replied softly, hoping to calm him. Besides, if she raised her voice, she would wake Tullia and alert her to the gravity of the situation. "I found you both like this. Let me help."

She reached for his hand and clutched it lightly. He did not have the strength to pull away.

"I am not here to get revenge either," she continued. "You disowned me when I chose to follow Jesus. But my decision to follow Him is what has made this miracle possible. You need me, and you need a miracle of your own." Shoshan looked at him, hoping he could read everything in her face.

He said nothing. As long as he remained silent, he conserved his strength. Perhaps it was good that he was not arguing.

Marcus had resented the disruption Jesus caused among the religious leaders and wealthy ruling class. Disruptions equaled a loss of income, because they demanded so much attention to resolve.

The Romans didn't care about theology, not at all. They cared about peace, because peace meant money.

The Romans were indulgent of many mystery religions, even offshoots of Judaism. But Jesus had quickly established Himself as something far different from those. He claimed to be the Son of God. No one had heard of the Jewish God having a son. All the known mythologies had gods with sons, mothers, and daughters, but the Hebrew God? No. He was called the "one true God."

The Sadducees had been in an uproar. The Roman officials did not like uproars. Marcus did not like seeing the Roman officials upset and knowing his sister was a part of it.

"I am not here to prove my faith either," she continued. "I will stay and help, even if you reject Jesus. You do not have to accept Him to accept my help."

His cold gaze flicked back to her, but a hint of the old Marcus was there. He was still her big brother, and he had always been so curious about the world, so quick to see an opportunity. He had never realized that she was his opposite. She had only wanted to make a quiet little home and stay there, forever, safe from the world. She didn't look at him or this situation as an opportunity for personal gain.

He had to know the truth if he was going to accept help. Marking his steady breathing, his open eyes…she judged him ready, as ready as a man near death could be, for such a heartbreak.

"You and Tullia have the Roman plague."

He nodded. Relief flooded her veins. It was not the shock she expected. He must have already guessed. His eyes cut to Tullia, and one eyebrow arched weakly.

"The baby lives," she said quickly. "But all your servants have left you."

She omitted the part about them looting the estate. What good would that do? At least now he understood how serious his situation was, and that she was all he had left.

"You were alone when I arrived, and I am trying to save you both," she said. "I cannot bring a doctor, not without risking a quarantine. I must be able to go in and out to bring food and medicine if there is any hope for you."

"We went to Greece," Marcus said, his voice faint. "To visit the temples there. Tullia's idea. To ask for a blessing from the gods for her pregnancy."

"What happened in Greece?" Shoshan asked, confused.

"The air was bad. Mosquitoes everywhere. We fell ill on the return ship. Made it home before anyone guessed. Tullia says a demon followed us. You could send for a sorcerer."

"No, absolutely not," Shoshan said, blinking, trying to absorb the story. Why would Tullia pray to foreign gods when she was the niece of the Jewish high priest? Shoshan resisted the urge to blame Tullia for the disease, though. It would do no good. Shame never did.

A boy's voice, high and sweet, rang through the air in a language she did not know.

Marcus turned his head toward the bedroom door.

"A servant I hired," she explained, patting Marcus's hand with a soft smile. "Try to rest now. He is boiling tea from a plant said to help these fevers. It should be ready soon, but it is bitter. I will fight this disease as if it were my own life threatened, but I will not call for a sorcerer."

"Your life *is* threatened," Marcus said, his eyes closing.

That was true. She had no way of knowing whether she would contract the disease. If she did, they might all die together. And what about little Haraka? If she ever needed to talk to Jesus, it was now.

She stood and stretched, watching as Marcus's breathing became deeper. His chest rattled every few seconds.

Noises from downstairs made her freeze, the muscles all over her body tightening all at once. Hooves stamped in the street below, and sounds of boots marching up to the entrance thundered in her ears.

Fear ran like a hot blade through her stomach. Marcus was asleep, or unconscious, she didn't know which.

"Open the gates!" a man commanded.

Haraka appeared at the top of the stairs, his eyes wide with terror.

"A man is outside the gates. He is surrounded by a small army."

CHAPTER FIFTEEN

Shoshan grabbed Tullia's veil and outer robe from the doorway and hurried down the steps. Sweeping the veil over her hair so that it fell at an angle across her face, she descended only far enough to see the gates clearly. Haraka followed behind her, asking questions faster than she could think.

Peering across the courtyard, she saw no red plumes or flashes of bronze.

"They are not guards," she said over her shoulder. Squinting, she could only make out the man who stood at the gates, his hands wrapped around the bars. He had a scruffy, unkempt beard and hair.

"Definitely not Roman," she murmured. The Romans were fastidious in their appearance. She looked over her shoulder to tell Haraka to wait on the stairs quietly.

But before she could turn her head, the lightning-fast boy was already at the foot of the stairs and striding confidently toward the gate. Shoshan pressed a hand to her mouth, wanting to call him back. She hadn't explained the entire situation to him. Haraka only knew she was caring for her brother, who was ill with the fever that the Romans feared above all others. She had omitted the part about how the Romans were hunting for her, how she had recently been dead, then brought back to life by a renegade rabbi the Jewish leaders had murdered. He was walking the streets as well, still bearing the marks of His crucifixion. Every day, her story seemed to grow in complexity. How could she possibly be expected to unravel the entire thing when she had just met this boy?

But now, if Haraka let those men through those gates, not understanding the danger they presented…

"What is your business?" Haraka called.

Haraka gave a shockingly good impersonation of a wealthy man's servant, she realized. He was acting. It hit her, like she was in an audience watching a performance. She had met him outside the doors to Herod's Theater. Haraka was a theater performer of some kind, maybe a member of a Greek chorus, but homeless and apparently an orphan. Yet, he was perfect in this role, that of an honorable house manager.

Haraka spoke to the man at the gates, but Shoshan could not hear their conversation. The man looked up and spied Shoshan on the stairs. He backed up a pace and nodded in deference to her. *He thinks I am Tullia. We are all actors today.* Pulling the veil closer across her face, she acknowledged him with a dip of her chin.

Haraka turned and dashed up the stairs to her.

"I need to offer him money."

She peered again at the man at the gate. "Why?"

"He has a delivery for us. Do not fret. It is paid for. We will give money, and his men will bring it inside the gates." Haraka shifted his weight from foot to foot. "Hurry."

Shoshan swallowed the next question she had and hurried back up the stairs to the coins.

On the stairs, the boy held out his palm, flat. She thrust the coins she had taken, all of them, into his hand. "I do not know how much to pay them."

She watched from the stairs as Haraka opened the gates. The man directed the others to bring in a cart loaded with several large crates. Drying racks. Meat. Her knees nearly buckled with the thought. The boy sorted through the coins, his back turned to the men, then paid them, each one receiving a coin. It must have been an appropriate wage, because the men eyed the coins with scowls but did not linger once they'd slipped them into their belts.

When the gates were closed, she was so astonished that she barely felt her feet touching the stairs as she descended. God had provided. It had nearly made her faint from fear, but He had provided, even after she had a fit of frustration after the market.

"Apparently, the master of the house has a standing order at the butcher's," Haraka said, heaving a crate up and carrying it toward the kitchen.

Of course he does. Shoshan laughed to herself. He probably had parties every week.

Parties! Fear returned, needling deep into her bones. Parties meant guests, including friends, the sort of people who would notice if he didn't make an appearance soon.

Here she was, holding the answer to a prayer for one problem, realizing another problem had already taken its place.

"I never thanked you," Shoshan said suddenly, turning to look at Haraka, who had returned to pick up another crate. "You have saved me and this household in ways I cannot explain right now."

His face brightened. "I can stay? I have a job, then?"

Hesitating, she knew she couldn't speak for Marcus, but would Marcus even live?

"On one condition," she replied.

"Anything."

"You must tell me your real name," she said.

He sighed, a heavy sound, like a struggle to shift the weight of a burden he carried.

"I do not have one," he said. After looking around, his attention snapped back to her. "If someone asks where all the servants are, what am I to say?"

She hadn't told him about the looting either. "They are alive and well, if you are worried about that."

He relaxed slightly, the tension in his face slowly softening.

"None of them died of the plague?" he asked, more curious than afraid.

She shook her head. "I assume that when my brother grew too sick and weak to defend himself, they stole everything and left."

Haraka blew a puff of air, moving his bangs out of his field of vision.

"If someone demands to see the master of the house," he asked, "what should I do?"

He had a lot of questions, challenges she hadn't even thought of yet. Together, they stared up at the second floor of the home. He was right to be worried about people demanding to see Marcus. That would be their undoing.

He was wise to think so far ahead. She looked back down at him, tender warmth enveloping her. Was this what it would have been like to be a mother here on earth?

She would never know. This boy needed her though.

"You are not just fast on your feet, Haraka." She tapped her temple, winking. "You have a fast mind."

She rested a hand on his shoulder. He shook it off and stepped back.

Bewildered, she watched as he set back to his task. If she had offended him, she could not think of a reason why.

Maybe she was not the only one in this house with secrets.

That next day, Marcus and Tullia slept after drinking a bit of broth. The heat of the afternoon was just beginning, and Shoshan sat beside the pool to rest for a moment. She was not used to the hard work of nursing two people at once.

She wanted to go and find Jesus. Was He still in Jerusalem, or was He going to wander the countryside like He did before the crucifixion? If Marcus and Tullia lived, they would have no more need of her. Antonius would not want her back, not since he had Miriam now. Maybe she would join His followers if they had regrouped.

The future was a painful thought. She had no home to return to, thanks to her husband and former best friend. And she did not belong here. Marcus had disowned her. Tullia lived in luxury like she had never known and was loved in a way Shoshan would never feel.

Shoshan shook her head. *Stop!* The warring thoughts were more dangerous than the Roman plague and only made her feel depressed and weak when she needed all her strength.

She forced herself to focus on the good things around her. There was meat in the kitchen, plenty of it. Haraka was in the kitchen right now working on a recipe from the Spartans, one that used a liberal amount of blood for seasoning and its properties of giving strength to the eater. Shoshan had shuddered when he told her of it, but if the Spartan warriors ate it and grew strong, then perhaps it was worth trying. And maybe over dinner the boy would share more of his story. He must have traveled to many places with the theater troupe.

The crackling of the kitchen fire was a comforting sound, and the scent of freshly baked bread wafted in the air. She wondered how long Haraka had been awake and working. He'd accomplished more in the first hours of the morning than she ever could.

He was a marvel. If Marcus recovered, he would be a fool to let him go.

Just then, a noise from beyond the gates made her body freeze with fear. She heard the clang of Roman armor and the tread of boots that approached.

Haraka walked from the kitchen, right out the gates, before she could stop him. He carried bread in his arms. She couldn't chase after him to stop him, not without showing her face. Ducking behind a tree, she spied. Neither of the guards looked familiar.

"My master sends these," Haraka said, standing in the street, tilting his head toward the home. "He appreciates how you keep these streets safe."

The guards looked up, and their eyes brightened in recognition as they saw the home. Marcus must have a reputation in this section of the city.

"Give him our thanks."

Haraka wiped his hands on his apron and paused to lean against the gates, like he was just another house servant loafing around, wasting a moment of his master's time.

"Keeping you busy, is he?" A guard laughed.

"You need this bread more than us," the other guard added. "You have no more muscle than a twig. You are hardly big enough to wield a spoon."

"If he fell in a pot, who is to say someone would not use him as a ladle? You look about the same size and shape," the first guard replied. They laughed at their own jokes, but Haraka only smiled.

Shoshan's anger blazed up, though. Haraka had just fed these two men, and they were mocking him.

Haraka continued his good-natured demeanor. "Master Marcus works night and day for the Roman empire, it is true. He expects nothing less from his servants. Maybe if he ever takes a break from the government, I will have a chance to rest. But not today." He put his hand on the gate, then looked back. "Oh, he hired new servants. The old ones stole from him."

"Should we take a report?" the first guard asked, much more attentive now.

"No," Haraka replied. "Let them try to find work without a reference from my master. They will soon be washing floors in the latrines."

The guards shuddered. Romans used open-air public latrines, which offered no privacy, but the cleanliness was remarkable. The benches and floors were cleaned every hour. Romans were a strange combination of a lack of modesty and a passion for order and good hygiene.

Haraka shut the gate as he walked back into the estate, leaving the men to tear at the bread with their teeth as they imagined if there could be a fate worse than that. They walked down the street, and Shoshan waited to emerge from her hiding spot until they were gone.

Then she laughed, the first pure laugh of this, her second life. It rose like a bubble in her throat and burst out. Haraka, the fast boy. How many times had she heard people complain that God was slow? He might seem to be at times, but His servants could shock you with their speed. God probably found such delight in this boy. She opened her mouth, wanting to call out and tell him that, then stopped. Praise seemed only to darken his mood.

She hoped there would be enough time to understand why.

CHAPTER SIXTEEN

Nursing Marcus and Tullia took all Shoshan's waking hours. Their condition did not improve, or at least not by much, but oddly, she was regaining her strength. Had she even been aware of how weak the terror and uncertainty of the last few days had left her? The act of caring for her brother had melted away any trace of resentment she had carried over from her previous life. Caring for Tullia was a continual sacrifice, but she felt called to this work, if only because there was no one else who would do it. The rabbis taught that humankind's only hope was the Lord, but the Lord often sent people to do His work.

She was on assignment from the Lord, she was sure of that. What surprised her the most, she supposed, was that God had resurrected her and given her a new life but hadn't changed her circumstances. Apparently, this second life did not include a perfect body or a perfect nature. Bitterness was still a temptation to be fought. She constantly had to choose between her old resentments and her new identity.

Jesus did not seem to suffer with this malady, she thought wryly. Else the guards who crucified Him would have feared for their lives when He walked into Jerusalem on the third morning. But He slipped quietly into the city, looking for the ones He loved.

The earthly fate of Marcus and Tullia was undetermined, but there was a chance for them to know Jesus. What Roman or Greek physician in this city would minister to them in this way? God had provided the right treatment for body and soul. The thought gave her courage. If God was this kind to them, surely He had plans for them that extended beyond this illness. Surely He was going to heal them.

Sitting beside the pool was becoming her favorite spot to rest. She settled there, dipping her toes into the cool water, and studied the blue and green tiles that lined the pool walls. Each was no bigger than the tip of her thumb. It must have taken the men hours of painstaking work to cut each stone. She wondered if their backs hurt at the end of the day. Antonius always complained of a backache after doing small stonework.

Tears stung her eyes. They had been happy once, hadn't they? Why had he betrayed her? When had the thought first entered his mind? Was it something she said or did, a grievance he secretly held against her? Or was it a longing unfulfilled, a quality or attribute she lacked that Miriam had, and he finally could not resist?

A raven fluttered, landing in the tree behind her, seeking refuge from the bright afternoon sun. She could hear the rustle of the branches and the harsh scolding as it called out. Peeking over her shoulder, she admired the sheen of its feathers. No amount of dye could ever create a garment so dark, and yet they glistened and caught the light so that it skimmed across the surface of the feathers.

The raven called again, a haughty sound, and flew off. She watched it fly. An unclean animal, the biblical law said. Yet God sent the ravens to feed Elijah. Shaking her head, she returned her attention to the pool. It was hard to understand God's thoughts and ways.

Haraka plopped down beside her, surprising her.

The raven returned and landed not far from Haraka. It hopped along the edge of the tiled pool edge. When she raised her arm to shoo it away, Haraka stopped her. With his other hand, he dipped into his apron and produced a handful of crumbs. Those he tossed lightly at the raven's feet. After a brief flutter, the bird calmed and began to eat.

He is kind to animals. His heart is still tender.

"No one cares for the ravens," Haraka said. "But they have to eat too."

"I know the one who cares for the birds," she said.

Haraka glanced up at her, one eyebrow arched. "All birds?"

She nodded.

"Hmph. He must be rich. And live in a faraway land, one that no one has ever visited." Haraka was dismissing the thought of anyone being kind and rich as a children's tale.

"Actually, I have met Him." She leaned in and whispered conspiratorially. "He fed me lunch one day when I had nothing to eat and was hungry. There were about five thousand of us, as the men count."

Men counted crowds by the number of men present. It was a habit everyone was accustomed to. Did the women and children not matter, or did the men even see them?

Haraka flopped his head back, making a silly, guttural sound. "That story is only fit for the stage! Even then the audience wouldn't believe it."

Shoshan laughed at his dramatics and poked him in the ribs with her elbow. "You are the one who is fit for the stage."

The raven cawed, as if scolding them for forgetting it was there. Haraka turned his apron pocket inside out, letting the remaining crumbs fall into his palm. He tossed them to the raven. Then he drew his legs up and turned to face her. He crossed his legs and rested his head on his hands, listening.

"I like your stories," he said. "Tell me about this man who cares for birds and women who forget their lunch."

Shoshan pressed her lips together, thinking back. How many things had she seen? How much had she heard? Her memory of that time with Jesus was like a box filled with shimmering, intertwined ropes of gold. She didn't know where one ended and another began. It was all riches.

Knowing Marcus and Tullia would sleep a while longer, she told him about the memory closest to her heart, how Jesus, the king of her people, held children and blessed them. Haraka liked it very much, the thought of a king who loved children. He had never heard of a king who loved anything but war.

As the sun stretched itself across the sky, she shared all she could remember. All that she had witnessed and all she had been taught growing up seemed to meet in Jesus, like two seams of a garment. When she told Haraka the story of Elijah and the ravens, and then the story of Jesus promising that every little sparrow is accounted for, he glanced up, scanning the courtyard.

The raven was gone.

"Too bad. He would have liked that story, I think," Haraka said, standing for a stretch. "I have to finish preparing supper."

Haraka needed care, just as much as Marcus and Tullia, but his medicine would be her words. *No, his medicine is Jesus.* That was all that she had to offer anyone. Jesus could send people and arrange interventions, but in the end, the only thing that saved was Jesus.

The thought encouraged her. The burden of trying to save Marcus and Tullia was heavy.

Shoshan stood too and walked to the stairs to check on her patients.

Haraka paused before he entered the kitchen and called out. "When I met you in the market, you looked afraid. Here, it seems safe enough, but you still jump anytime there is a loud noise on the street outside. What do I need to know?"

That my husband murdered me, and then I came back to life, and now he might try again to silence me forever? That Roman guards are hunting for me and will arrest me on sight, if they do not kill me in a dark alleyway first just to keep the peace?

Tapping her forefinger to her temple, she sighed, making Haraka laugh. He could think as fast as he could run, and he seemed to need her to notice that, and to notice him. But she was not ready to answer his questions, because he might not be ready for the truth. She turned around quickly before he could read her face again.

She did not want him to see that she was afraid to die again, at the hands of either Antonius or the Roman guards. And did she want to die of the Roman plague?

But Jesus had reminded her that death was nothing to be afraid of.

Maybe the fight she faced now was not to stop feeling the fear but to start remembering what He said.

Marcus was sitting upright in bed, his eyes focused on the stairs, waiting for her.

And she felt that familiar tremble of panic, being his little sister. Marcus had somehow always known what Shoshan had been up to, and how much trouble he could cause for her if he chose. Growing up, she'd had a fondness for sneaking little animals into the house, wild babies that could fit in her palm, who had managed to scramble away from some terrible disaster. She had always been so determined to save them, but nature always won. Nature was death, Marcus had told her.

Now Marcus was a great man in the Roman empire, and the nature of Rome was nothing less than the same. It was death, even if it prized itself on being orderly.

"What month is it?" he asked, his chest rising and falling sharply.

"Nisan," she replied, walking to the bedside table. She referred to the month using the Hebrew calendar and saw his eyes quickly glance up as he bit his lower lip. It was a familiar mannerism, one she had seen on his face many times in childhood, especially when practicing his math.

"March, then?" he murmured.

Had he really left it all behind? Was he Roman now to his core?

After dipping a linen into the water on the table, she dabbed at his forehead.

"The last thing I remember," he rasped, "was my house manager asking for extra allowance. Passover was approaching. Leaven would be hard to find for a few days."

"True, and then our celebrations would make it hard to find anyone to sell it," she grinned. Although Passover was a holiday that was distinct and limited to seven days, the spirit of happiness lasted all month. Nisan was the head of the year, the first month of the new year. True, the Hebrews had four such months, but Nisan was the most joyful. It was called the month of the king, and was the month that God led the people out of Egypt, the month when the tabernacle was first shown to the people. Nisan was the dawn of spring. It meant winter was over. Everywhere you looked, new life broke through the still-cold ground.

Is that why Jesus chose that month to die and be resurrected?

"Shoshan?"

She blinked and looked at her brother. "I am sorry. Did I miss a question?"

"How bad is it?" he asked again.

"You are healing." She looked at Tullia. "And Tullia's color is certainly better. The baby is alive, so there is hope."

"I mean…are there others?"

"In the city?" she asked, then understood. He thought this was part of an epidemic. If it were, Rome would be sending aid and the best physicians by now. Marcus's hope was in the Roman empire, but she knew the empire would not be coming to save him.

The empire used him when he was alive, but would it care if he died? He was easily replaced. Every man wanted to become a patrician.

Seeing the gleam of hope in his eyes, she hesitated. The best she could do for him was to give him the truth at all times. Maybe not the entire truth all at once, but bitter truth in small doses was still better medicine than pleasant lies.

"No one else in the city is sick," she said. "Not to my knowledge."

A shadow passed over his face. His dreadful circumstances must be revealing themselves to him, like a specter appearing in the windows. How terrified he would be as the truth sank in. She rested a hand on his arm. It was hot, like an iron just pulled from the fire.

The afternoon fever had returned, it seemed. Why did the fever come and go like this? It raged in the morning, then left, only to return in the afternoon. If only there was a physician she could consult...

"My servants have all fled." His voice was flat as he stared at the wall behind her.

She nodded. Was he ready for the truth, all of it?

"Are we quarantined?" His gaze flicked back to her face.

"No. I have a boy named Haraka who is helping run the house. Together, he and I maintain the illusion that all is normal here. But we are alone. I do not know how long it can last."

"A boy?" Marcus asked.

"He is about thirteen years of age, I think," she replied.

In Roman law, a male without a father was not considered a man until his twenty-fifth birthday. But a father could always declare his son to be an adult after the age of fourteen. Haraka had no father, so he would not be recognized as a man for many years yet.

She had said more than she meant to, but Marcus seemed stronger today. The meat broth was giving him energy, and the wormwood tea seemed to be controlling his fevers. Still, she wondered how much to tell him. He had been absent from her life for nearly three years. They were strangers to each other in many respects.

"Where is Jesus?" Marcus asked.

"He was crucified, remember? And I told you what happened after that." Shoshan did not know how much Marcus remembered from day to day after each conversation, or if he would survive with his mind intact.

Marcus frowned, annoyed. "I remember. You said Jesus returned to life, along with some people who were His followers."

"No, I did not say that, not exactly. Not everyone who was raised had met Jesus." She thought of the man who saw the wall built under Nehemiah's leadership. "Some people lived hundreds of years ago. They had never heard or seen Jesus, not in their first life."

Marcus fixed his gaze on her. "I need to understand the purpose of these stories that you are repeating. Are His followers preparing for vengeance for the crucifixion? Plotting against Caesar? Tullia and I will be executed for harboring you."

"No, there is no plot or plan for revenge," Shoshan said. "Jesus was raised to life, but He revealed no sort of plan or plot. Believing in Him, that is all He has said to do next."

Marcus scoffed. "You were always so naive. No one goes to so much trouble if they do not have a plan."

The accusation was like a sword through her heart. She sat back, dazed, unable to even look at him. She had been naive, long ago, but what had happened to her as a child on the streets of Rome had ended her innocence. That had been his fault. They had never spoken of that terrible event, never. But he knew, surely, why the family had to leave Rome.

Marcus gestured for the cup, and she pressed it to his lips, waiting as he drank broth. Her knuckles clenched the cup as she tried to remain calm. She did not want to speak of the past, not about that day at least. Not ever.

Marcus sighed. "So, either Tullia and I die alone, or we die with you. Or we die because of you. Where is the scenario in which we live? What is the point of you even being here, Shoshan, if your presence will doom us?"

"You need me," Shoshan replied flatly. "So does Tullia. I have worked tirelessly to care for you, but I cannot promise we will not all succumb to this disease. As for the guards..."

She had no answer for that.

"I will allow you to stay and take care of us only as long as my wife continues to improve. If she dies, I will turn you into the guards myself."

Shoshan's mouth opened, but she had no immediate reply, except a short laugh.

"Do I control this disease?" she asked, frustration at his ingratitude creeping into her voice. "No. And it does not care about your money. Besides, you have nothing here to negotiate with. Your servants looted your house. Even if you sent word to Rome to empty your treasury accounts and send the money here, you might not be alive by the time the funds arrived."

His eyes flared in anger, but she continued. She was too tired and too afraid to restrain herself any longer.

"I am here because I was dead, and now I am alive. The One who raised me asked me to come and care for you. You will have to decide, brother, who Jesus is and why He sent me to you. Do you think I am a madwoman who imagined it all? Or a woman bent on revenge? If not, then you must concede that the impossible has happened and everything I have told you is the truth."

He studied her for a long moment in silence. Then, lifting a trembling hand, he held out his hand to her, palm down.

She hesitated, unsure of what he expected. Was she supposed to kiss his hand, as if he was her ruler?

"My seal," he whispered, his eyes shutting briefly. Her eyes focused on the ring on his first finger. It was a wonder that the servants had not stolen that too, but they would have had to cut it off his finger.

"What do I do?" she asked.

"Write a letter. Say that I am traveling and have left you and…"

"Haraka," she prompted.

"…Haraka in command until I return. Bring it to me. I will sign and seal it."

Relief flooded her body, a feeling like warm water being poured over her shoulders. Her entire body felt limp. No one would dare question Haraka if they stopped him on the street. That seal would protect them all for a little while longer.

Marcus managed a weak smile. "Authority has its advantages."

His eyes shut and did not reopen. Marcus had shown her mercy, but he was not ready to hear her story, not yet. Not about Antonius and not about Jesus, everything that He meant to her.

Which one would upset him more? That Antonius murdered her, or that she had a daughter in heaven and had held her? That everything he believed about Jesus, and God, was wrong? He was near death and had no idea who God really was or how to make peace with Him. Marcus had not even been able to make peace with her, especially not since that day in the streets of Rome so long ago.

"You rest," Shoshan said, pushing the memory away. "I am going to bring broth and bread. Haraka brewed a fresh batch of the medicine, but it is still cooling." She said nothing of the Spartan blood recipe. It sounded horrendous.

It did not matter, though. He did not seem to hear a word of it. Whether he knew she was there or not, she had work to do.

A recognition dawned in her mind. This was the work of her second life, was it not? There was no praise or acknowledgment, not even gratitude for most of her efforts, yet it felt good to do what needed to be done. Even if what needed to be done was saving the brother who had betrayed her. This was why she was given another chance to live, she was sure.

Of course, it would be different if Jesus had asked her to save Antonius, or even Miriam. But Jesus could not be that cruel, could He?

CHAPTER SEVENTEEN

Tullia felt well enough to sit up and sip broth from a bowl. The Sabbath had passed without any setbacks or fevers, and the baby seemed to be doing well.

Tullia's strength did not last long, but Shoshan was comforted. Her sister-in-law might survive. The baby might too. Pressing a hand to Tullia's abdomen, Shoshan felt a soft swish of the baby stirring. Tullia's eyes brightened. She must have felt it too.

Shoshan sat on the edge of her bed, broke off a piece of flatbread, and offered it to her. Tullia stared at it with a strained expression. She was too weak to take it from Shoshan's hand. Holding the bowl herself to drink from it had taken all her strength.

Shoshan set the bread down. Slowly, she reached and took the bowl from Tullia's hands and set it aside. After breaking off a smaller bit of bread, she pushed it gently between Tullia's lips. Tullia's jaw moved slowly. Her eyes met Shoshan's. Her mouth drew into a tight line that pulled at the edges, and she looked intently into Shoshan's eyes. Shoshan understood.

She is terrified for her baby.

"The baby is fine." Shoshan patted her hand. "You are both going to be all right. I'm going to stay and take care of you both. I will not leave."

Tullia stared at her, her deep brown eyes going over every detail of Shoshan's face.

"Do you remember me?" Shoshan asked. "I am Marcus's sister, Shoshan. Do you remember seeing me at your wedding?"

Three years ago? It seemed like a lifetime ago. Shoshan laughed softly. *It was.*

The marriage had been political at heart. Tullia, as the niece of the high priest, offered wealth of many kinds. Money, connections, and prestige, all of which Marcus must have found desirable, and she was beautiful. Shoshan remembered how her own breath caught when she first saw Tullia. Her smooth skin, wide brown eyes, and black hair with its perfect curls. Even if Tullia had been born poor, she would have been a prize men fought over.

Marcus had been in love, certainly, and Shoshan saw that. She had hoped that love would change him, and soften his heart.

By the day of the wedding, Shoshan had been following Jesus for several months. Marcus had warned her not to speak of Jesus to anyone at the wedding. His name caused indignation among the temple leaders and political dignitaries. Rome was weary of Jewish uprisings. Jesus would be just another in a long line of rebels who caused great suffering and embarrassment for his people, Marcus said. Do not get caught in His web.

In the end, she was allowed to attend the wedding but only as a guest, not a member of the family. Antonius was denied the right to circulate among the more honored guests. He was outraged. His hopes of business contacts and better-paying work vanished, all thanks to her fascination with this countryside preacher named Jesus.

Shoshan knew that Tullia was aware of her presence at the wedding, but Marcus had forbidden her to speak to or even acknowledge Shoshan. Even then Marcus had treated Tullia as a treasure to be hoarded, walled off from the world. He refused to let Shoshan contaminate her with ideas about Jesus.

After the exchange of vows, the servants at the wedding worked quickly, packing a small bit of food and sending Shoshan and Antonius away. They were not even allowed to stay for the feast. It was an insult that took her breath away.

The following month, when she paid a visit to bless Tullia and Marcus, to pray for their union as a new husband and wife, she found the gates locked, as if someone had spied her approach and taken action. The house manager told her that Marcus had no living sister. The cold look in his eye was one she had never forgotten.

Marcus had eliminated all traces of her, if only in his imagination. How convenient for his political ascent in Rome. Especially since the family name might cause some to remember the scandal that involved Shoshan and a certain son of the emperor. If Marcus had no sister, the scandal would never be connected to him.

But at this moment, Shoshan was Marcus's only lifeline to the outside world, and his best chance to save his little family. Shoshan looked down at Tullia, her frail body fighting for her unborn baby.

Tullia's eyes narrowed, and then she smiled briefly, managing one slight nod. *Yes*, she seemed to say. *I do remember you, that day, my wedding.*

The fever had not left her with permanent brain damage, praise God. Shoshan had heard stories of that.

"I remember your wedding finery," Shoshan said. "The veil from Italy, the fabric so delicate, it was like the wings of a butterfly shimmering underneath the sun."

Tullia smiled, remembering. It must have been a good day for her. Marcus must be a good husband. He must really love her.

"There was a rabbit in the courtyard that day, did you know that?" Shoshan asked. "He watched you walk to Marcus, and his little nose twitched the whole time you said your vows. He looked jealous that Marcus won your heart."

Tullia laughed, a little whoosh of air.

"I think that rabbit is still in the courtyard," Shoshan said. "When you feel better, we will go together and look for him, all right? Maybe he has found a wife and has children of his own now."

She rested a hand on Tullia's belly. "The baby's moving! Do you feel it? I think you are going to have a big, healthy baby!"

Tullia studied Shoshan's face carefully.

Was Tullia looking for signs that Shoshan was lying to her? These stories, these cheerful remembrances, were just to encourage Tullia. Shoshan could not promise that the baby and Tullia would both survive, could she? But hope was the strongest medicine Shoshan had to offer right now, she was sure of that.

Finally, Tullia blinked and smiled, and the panic that had etched itself into her face earlier was gone.

How frustrating for Tullia to be this weak, and how humbling. She once commanded the servants of this house. She did not have to raise her voice back then. She only had to lift a finger to point, and it was done. Now she could not even speak or point. And she had no servants. They had all betrayed her.

Shoshan and Tullia were more alike now than ever.

"You need to eat and drink all you can. The baby needs to put on weight before he or she arrives," Shoshan told her with a confidence she did not feel. Tullia's birthing story would end differently than her own. What good was all this pain otherwise?

Resting the back of her hand against Tullia's cheek, she was relieved that the fever was not as high as it had been in days past. She gave Tullia a sip of broth, then a tiny bit of bread between her lips, cupping her chin to help her eat.

"And you will want to be thinking of names," Shoshan said cheerfully, though her stomach clenched with nerves. Tullia was eating, which was a good sign. But she was far too weak. If she did go into labor early, she would never have the strength to deliver the child. They would both die.

And Marcus? He'd never want to see Shoshan again. He would kick her out, and she would fall into the hands of Antonius or the guards.

"Marcus," Shoshan said over her shoulder. Marcus sipped his broth and watched Tullia with concentrated urgency. It was as if he was willing Tullia to take every bite.

"When is Tullia due? Do you remember the exact date?"

Marcus looked down, thinking. "Just before the wheat harvest. That is why we traveled."

Tullia looked at him, and her face lit, just for an instant, like a curtain pulled away from a window at noon. Then the curtain fell, and her face took on its pallor of the afflicted.

Shoshan bit her lip, calculating. "So just before the Feast of Weeks." That gave Tullia about five weeks. Of course, dates could be wrong. And babies came early or late. Just the thought of five weeks, the numbers themselves ringing through her mind, was encouraging. Shoshan had time to nurse Tullia and get her strong enough to deliver.

A sickening twist in her gut hit, as surely as if someone had slipped a knife there. Would Tullia's baby be born alive? Like a great dark current, a flood of memories hit Shoshan. The pain of labor, the rippled heat of contractions across her abdomen, the copper scent of blood, the midwife's supplies on the bedstand, the flash of the blade that severed the cord.

A storm cloud of silence had filled the room. Shoshan remembered it now, whether it was possible or not. A thunderous silence that pressed against the walls and ceiling as if to burst the house in its need for breath, for noise, for a baby's cry.

Shoshan closed her eyes, pressing them hard until she saw colors behind her eyelids. The memories from that day and that room could not affect her judgment. Tullia had to see her behaving as if everything was going to be all right, as if there was no other possible outcome but joy.

There is a world where that is true. But that world is not ours. Not yet.

———

Torches lit the street outside the gates. The stench of rendered fat and fresh entrails clotted the air, worrying Shoshan. Marcus and Tullia were not strong enough to fight one more illness. Disease was caused by bad air. Everyone knew that. Why, then, did the Roman government allow these magicians and sorcerers to parade through the streets at night, practicing their dark rituals? She found large parchment fans and, with Haraka's assistance, fanned Marcus and Tullia, driving the stench from the room.

Tullia murmured, her sleep fitful. Marcus was half awake, his eyes opening and shutting at slow, unpredictable intervals. They must be used to this, but Shoshan was not. The sorcerers never paraded through the poorer streets of Jerusalem. Why not? Because there was no money there to charm away from its owner? Or because they only wanted the elite to find a way into the afterlife?

Oh, how this city had needed Jesus. He had overturned more than the tables in the temple. He had upended everything these sorcerers of Rome taught about deep spiritual secrets. The dark magicians would stand in the market, calling out for "those who are born with the gift, come and hear." Only a select few, those with the gift of supernatural abilities, were allowed to listen to their teaching. Shoshan suspected they targeted anyone born with money. But then along came Jesus, who called out His outrageously simple message: "Those who have ears, come and hear." Anyone was welcome to come and hear Him.

Was that the moment she had first loved Him? Maybe. There were so many moments like that. She was not the only one who felt that either. Anywhere He went, His presence was like lightning that traveled underground. People sensed something happening, something beyond all their known experience. For many, that alone was good news.

Outside, she heard the sorcerers chanting. *Move along*, she willed them. Rome had such high tolerance for "mystery religions" as the government referred to them. The real mystery was why intelligent people indulged. Did they not see that Rome found these endless permutations useful? A people who could not agree on truth created chaos, and chaos demanded a tyrant. Rome filled the void admirably.

"Passover is over?" Marcus's voice, barely a soft scratch, interrupted her thoughts. She turned from the window, still holding the fan, to face him.

"Yes," she reminded him. They'd discussed dates already. His mind was not working well. Had the fever left a permanent void in his memory, an inability to hold onto details from day to day? "Passover was about two weeks ago."

She'd been dead two weeks ago. How was this life real? It seemed more like a dream. And she had yet to tell Marcus her entire story, though that was understandable. He could not keep track of simple things like days and time. What would he think if he knew Antonius had murdered her? What sense would he make of her resurrection after such a crime, especially since she had no desire for revenge? She looked away, wondering when the time would be right to tell him about Antonius and the affair, and her daughter. Maybe never. If he was going to die, why burden him now with a story he would not be able to understand?

"Wealthy men from Turkey come after Passover." Marcus gestured weakly to the window, explaining the ghoulish celebration in the street. "The sorcerers are for them." The noises were, mercifully, fading.

"The sorcerers love to put on quite a show," Haraka mumbled. He stood on the other side of Tullia's bed, fanning her.

Marcus strained to see him.

"Marcus, this is Haraka, the boy who is helping us now," Shoshan said. A flutter of fear passed through her stomach. Marcus would never approve of a street beggar or a theater performer serving as his housemaster. But approval was no longer an option. He was not the master of his family, not any longer. The disease was.

She breathed deeply, pushing the breath into her stomach. His situation and having a total stranger as a new house manager was a difficult reality for Marcus to navigate. Haraka was just a child, really, if someone looked past his bravado. Would Marcus be able to face all this without a mental collapse, a fit of anger and confusion?

"Where are your people from?" Marcus asked Haraka.

Shoshan inhaled again and waited.

"Northern tip of Africa. The Phoenicians started a colony there." Haraka answered without fear or shame, meeting Marcus's gaze.

"I know it well," Marcus replied, groaning a bit as he shifted in his bed. "I trade with the merchants who sail from there."

"What do you buy?" Haraka cried and dropped his fan. Shoshan held out a hand to stop him, seeing he was poised to lunge at Marcus. He looked as if he would throw himself across the bed in his anger. His temper was as quick as his feet.

"Pearls." Marcus cocked his head. "I have heard there are slave ships, but I abhor slavery."

Haraka picked up his fan, face downcast. "The Romans keep slaves," he muttered, arguing.

Shoshan looked between the two, unsure if she should stop Haraka before he lost his job and doomed them all. Where else would she find a house manager willing to serve in a home infected with the plague?

"Romans provide a way for any slave to earn his or her freedom," Marcus replied. "Even so, I have never owned slaves. I was born a Hebrew."

Shoshan watched Haraka's face to see if he understood. His face remained impassive.

"I will explain to you in depth later, Haraka," she said, her body relaxing. Somehow, it knew the danger had passed even before her mind comprehended it. Haraka's challenge had been resolved peaceably just as fast as he had raised it. No wonder Marcus rose quickly to power in government. He handled opponents so easily. She turned to Haraka to explain her brother's reference to being a Hebrew. The boy still looked skeptical, as if he had been fooled and was not sure how.

"It has to do with Passover," she said. "The celebration we just had here in Jerusalem. You will like the story. It might bring you comfort when you think about your mother. And might explain why Jesus chose this month to be crucified and resurrected. No one is meant to live as a slave. Jesus came to lead us out of slavery, forever."

It was a bold statement.

Marcus's face flushed a dark red. "How can any man choose the month he dies, unless he plans to die by his own hand? And you say He came back to life? It is trickery, all of it. You scoff at the sorcerers in the street, but you are no better. I do not want to hear any more talk of the dead." He coughed, his body shaking from the effort.

"I am not dead," Shoshan said. "I was raised."

"You belong to a cult. A dangerous cult," Marcus said.

She rested the fan on the bed. The smell was not so bad now, and the noise from the street had quieted.

"Haraka, could you go and prepare more broth?" she asked. He exited at once, probably sensing the tension between brother and sister.

"Do you think you could take a little more broth before you sleep?" Shoshan asked Marcus. "It would help strengthen you."

Marcus shook his head, not looking at her. She had pushed him too far. He disliked Jesus more than she realized.

"I did not come here planning to convert you," she reassured him again. Her words fell to the ground like blind, flightless birds. "I only stayed because you and Tullia will not survive if I leave. And I will not leave, not until you are well again."

Unless the guards arrest me. Or Antonius finds me. Or I get sick too.

But this was not the time to talk about her problems. Reaching out with one hand, she braced herself against the wall. The brick was cool under her palm. Closing her eyes, she concentrated on the rough texture of the limestone, each bump and ridge like a language all its own encased in stone. The sensation brought comfort to her. Jerusalem still stood. Everything else had changed, fallen and risen, but these stones were still faithful, solid witnesses. The rock came from the land of David. Nehemiah. Solomon. They had seen Jesus enter these streets as its king at Passover. Jerusalem had endured so much. She could too.

"I will have Haraka bring some broth for Tullia. She needs to get as much nourishment as she can. For the baby's sake."

Marcus's gaze followed her as she exited, and it left her uneasy. He was different after their conversation, as if he had made a decision. She wondered what his choices had been.

She walked down the staircase, carefully picking her way by torchlight, his accusation still stinging. Her skin prickled, like invisible messengers of alarm racing back and forth, skimming the surface of her entire body.

Stopping on the staircase, she listened, trying to understand this feeling of panic. Then she heard a man's voice say her name.

"Shoshan?"

She looked up, toward the gate, squinting as the torches flickered and hissed.

Antonius had found her.

His eyes met hers, and he rubbed his hands together as if cleaning them before a task. Without saying a word, he slid back into the night, the sound of his footfalls swallowed by the croaks of frogs and the keening of insects.

He had a plan.

CHAPTER EIGHTEEN

Haraka," Shoshan said, surprised to find him asleep in the kitchen the next morning. She'd passed a restless night, keeping vigil on the stairs, watching the gates for Antonius's return, listening for any signs of distress from Marcus and Tullia. Haraka had not appeared, not even once. The conversation with Marcus had upset him more than she realized, perhaps.

"Why do you not sleep in the servants' beds?" she asked Haraka, trying her best to focus on him. He looked like a cat curled up in the corner. In reality, he was now the master of a very wealthy man's home. No one would believe a house manager slept like that, like a kitchen slave.

Haraka, still half-asleep, frowned when he looked up and saw her standing over him. He must have been embarrassed to be caught sleeping, but he needed rest. They all did.

She could not afford to, though. Her lonely watch through the night had been a waste, but she could not dwell on that. Antonius had not returned, but the quiet hours had given her time to think, time to come up with a plan.

Nothing had come together in her mind that made sense. What could she possibly do? Marcus was of no help to her. Using his seal to have Antonius arrested would not be much use if Marcus could not appear in court. Haraka was too young and not strong enough to fight off Antonius if Antonius decided to storm through the gates.

And neither Marcus nor Haraka knew why Antonius would be looking for her. Neither knew why he was such a dangerous man. Even if she went to the guards, even if she had Marcus's seal and demanded Antonius's arrest, what could she say? What was the charge against her husband?

This man murdered me. He also had an affair with my best friend, whom I cannot find right now. She will not admit that, but I caught them together when I walked back home from the cemetery in my grave clothes.

It would be laughable to them. Where was her proof? Antonius had not killed her, they would laugh. She was very much alive. How could she prove that she had been dead? She could not. The guards would be forced to ask Marcus if she needed to be sent away for a health cure, or simply sent into exile. And if the guards recognized her as one of the resurrected followers of Christ, she would be in terrible danger.

Oh, where is Jesus? If she ever needed Him, it was now. It was not enough to give her a second life if she did not know how to live it! Despair and guilt hovered around her like a storm cloud. She could not catch her breath.

She'd brought Antonius to their door, led him right to them. He was capable of murder. He was capable of anything. She had not told them, but she had put them in danger. She was keeping secrets. How was she any different than he was? Just because her motivation was different, just because she had not found the right time, did that make her less guilty? Her secret could kill them.

Haraka stretched. "It is warm in here, near the fire." He had bought a few more things on his last trip to market. She had assumed he would buy proper bedding for himself, since the servants had stolen that too. Only the straw mattresses remained, and if a servant had tried to steal those, well, someone would have asked questions.

"Last night, in the bedroom upstairs, what did Marcus say that upset you?" Shoshan asked.

Haraka stood and grabbed a spoon, choosing to stir the broth rather than answer.

She looked around the kitchen, at the fire in the grate, the steaming broth in a dented iron pot over the fire, the bread made last night resting on the wood block table. There were bundles of dried herbs hanging from the walls, affixed by nails, and several wood ladles with handles as long as Haraka's arm. He had spent the money entrusted to him on this kitchen, this task of caring for them.

He was making a home. The thought twisted her heart. He might not be able to keep it. No matter how hard he worked, or how much he wanted this, the future was uncertain. *God is merciful, but life is unfair.* She refused to voice her fears though. Somehow, she suspected he already understood.

She crossed the kitchen and rested her hand on his shoulder. This time, he did not resist.

"What did Marcus say that upset you?" she asked again, gently turning him to face her.

He released the ladle, letting it fall against the side of the pot.

"The ships," Haraka said. His chin jutted forward, daring her to argue, but she still had no idea what the insult was.

"Haraka, my brother and I are very different people. We have never agreed on much, even when we were children. Three years ago, he disowned me completely," she said. "Whatever trading he does, it has nothing to do with me."

"If he disowned you, what are you doing here?" He looked shocked.

"It is a long story, I suppose, why I came here," she replied. "But I saw the condition Marcus and Tullia are in. I had to stay. I had to help them."

"But Marcus disowned you. That is as good as being dead to him."

"Death has not stopped me so far," she murmured, hoping to find the humor in it, then watched as Haraka cocked his head, confused. She had to try again to explain why she had decided to stay.

"Haraka, my brother broke my heart, that is true. He caused me so much pain and embarrassment. And I should be angry with him. Maybe later, I will be. But right now, none of that matters. I must try to save him and Tullia."

"But even if you save him, he might not take you back as his sister. He could betray you again. Is that a risk you want to take? Not everyone is worth our time." Haraka was astute. He heard what she had not said. She had to do this, but she did not want to, not really. She wanted to be free of it all and be with her daughter.

But Jesus had given her this new life, and it was not hers to direct.

"Life is full of have-tos, is it not?" she said gently. "And you are right. Marcus is free to reject me again, no matter what happens. Just because I showed up here and have done my best to help him, that is no guarantee he will ever acknowledge me as his sister. I am not here because I have something to gain."

Haraka scowled. He lived in a world of transactions, where everything had to be earned or stolen.

"It is true," Shoshan replied softly. "I do not want to be here at all, but I was a follower of Jesus. Jesus is the Son of God, the God who cares for all the birds, remember?" She did not know if she should speak of her former life in the past tense. Was she still a follower of Jesus now that He no longer wandered the countryside? She had seen His crucified body, seen Him resurrected and free.

Would there be a different name for people like her now?

"I remember," Haraka nodded. "There was always trouble when He was in the city."

She smiled, but his words sent a chill down her spine.

"Why did Jesus want you to come back here?" Haraka asked suddenly. "For revenge?"

"No!" she replied. "I do not know why He sent me here, and I do not know why I have to stay alive. You see, I had a daughter, but she died. I want to be with her. Living without her is hard."

This was the first time she had told anyone in this house about her daughter. Marcus had heard rumors, but he did not know what happened. She had been unable, or unwilling, to tell him the story during that awful conversation earlier.

Haraka studied her, gnawing on his lower lip before relenting. His strength, the wall that kept him separate from her and from the world, crumbled all at once, and he suddenly looked smaller than he had the moment before. Smaller, and more fragile. Lunging toward her, he wrapped his arms around her and hugged her, then released her just as quickly.

"My mother fed beggars who came to our home in Africa," he began, wiping at his eyes with the back of his hands. "Everyone knew it. The sailors often had things to barter with, but not all. Some promised to return with riches to repay her great kindness. Day after day, I would sit on a bluff overlooking the docks, waiting for a ship to return bearing those riches. She had done many kindnesses. She deserved all the riches in the world."

"What happened?" Shoshan asked.

"One of the men she had cared for returned, yes. He said he had treasures on the ship and she could pick out whichever pleased her."

His face was lined with pain, remembering.

Shoshan waited.

"It was a neighbor who told me why she left," Haraka said. "I was on the bluff as usual that day. When I saw her getting on a ship, I did not know why. I knew it was high tide. I should have stopped her! She went below, into the hold, as if searching for something, and never returned above deck. The ship raised its sails when it hit open water and was gone."

He looked at Shoshan. "It was a slave ship. The sailor came for my mother. She was beautiful. Many men desired her. Now, somewhere, one man owns her."

The breath was knocked out of her, the cruelty like a blow to her stomach. Poor boy. And his mother. Shoshan refused to think of the horrors, if the mother was alive. It would be more merciful, perhaps, if she was not.

"What happened next?" Shoshan was afraid to ask if he knew where his mother was, because of course he could not. She was lost to him forever, disappearing on the waters, the sea swallowing her up, never to return her.

"Neighbors fed me for a while until one caught me stealing. I did not mean to hurt them. I was saving up for a voyage of my own, to find my mother, but they did not care. They sold me on the next ship leaving port."

"You were on a slave ship?"

"No," Haraka said. "I was a ship hand. But I overheard the captain's plans to sell me once we hit port, so as soon as we did, I ran. I was fast then too. And shorter. I was hard to catch."

Shoshan sighed. "You have had so much pain in your life."

Haraka drew himself up so that he was once more the brilliant, resourceful boy she knew best.

"I do not steal anymore. But I still save my money. Someday I will find that sailor who lied to my mother, and I will slit his throat."

She flinched as if his words were a band of pain cinched tight.

"Oh, Haraka, do not set your heart on revenge," she said. "Your mother would want you to be happy."

"Happiness was life with my mother," he replied flatly. "I do not know how to be happy without her."

"I understand," she replied. And she did.

He looked at her then, his eyes softening.

Her greatest sorrow was somehow the reason he could trust her with his own.

Maybe being together with Haraka at this moment in Shoshan's life was part of His plan. Haraka and she had both been betrayed, and both had suffered the death of a beloved one.

Haraka needed her, and she needed him. That was enough for now.

"When the broth is ready, take some to my brother, will you?" she asked.

"But what about you?" Haraka asked suddenly. "If you do not have your daughter, what will you live for? How will you find happiness?"

She hung her head. She had not told him her full story, nor Marcus. She had so much to tell them both, and to tell everyone, of her past and her experiences with Jesus. If she died before she told them, Antonius's version of the story would be remembered as the truth. It would be the only one told. It was important to tell her story. She saw that now.

She turned, ready to tell him. Haraka would be the first to hear the whole truth about her previous life, and how the man she loved murdered her. He would hear about Jesus and everything she had seen Him do.

Just then, a scream shattered the silence of the courtyard.

Shoshan and Haraka raced to the courtyard. Haraka's arm shot out, stopping her from proceeding any farther. Her heart thundered in her ears.

"The street," he whispered, pointing to the gates and the street beyond.

A flash of the red plume of a Roman guard was visible. A woman fought against him, but he grabbed her wrists and yanked both her arms behind her. She screamed in agony again as he forced her to her knees in the street.

Shoshan gently rested a hand on Haraka's arm and stepped away from him. Her stomach clenched as she approached the gate. Something about that woman's voice was familiar…

"Shoshan!" It was Miriam's voice.

The young guard with a scarred face looked up as Shoshan approached the gate. They locked eyes, and she watched as his eyes widened in recognition, then malice. She had eluded him once, his eyes seemed to say, but not this time.

She remembered overhearing his name. Clemens.

He had found her, his prize, the prey that had escaped his hunt.

She stared at Miriam, who stood next to him, wondering why her former friend was here. Guilt? A bounty for finding her?

"Open the gate," Clemens called to her.

Shoshan did not move.

Miriam twisted, trying to break his grasp and get away, but Clemens only tightened his grip as she struggled, until her knees left a dark streak on the stone. She was bleeding.

"What is her crime?" Shoshan demanded. She was at the gate now, her hands wrapped around the bars in a vice-like grip.

"Step into the street and I will tell you," Clemens offered.

"I am a Roman citizen," Shoshan announced. She watched as Clemens's face fell. This was a complication he had not expected. He could not break into the courtyard to arrest her. *He probably thinks only the local Jews follow Jesus. He forgets this is a city of surprises. Not everyone is what they appear.*

Especially Jesus. He was no ordinary carpenter.

Neighbors had come out at hearing the commotion. Shoshan saw faces of servants pressed between the iron bars. People peered from windows of the houses overlooking the street. Children had run up to their roofs to watch.

More soldiers arrived. She winced at the sound of the armor plates clanging, the heavy tread of military boots in the street. Dust swirled in the air, obscuring her view as soldiers gathered around Miriam.

"Shoshan, he is going to kill you! You are going to die!" Miriam was frantic as she fought the guards, but her panic seemed focused on Shoshan. Miriam was desperate to communicate something to her, even if it cost her life.

A soldier struck her across the back of the head. "Shut up, woman!"

"Stop!" Shoshan yelled. The soldiers looked at her. She knew what they saw. A wealthy man's wife in a fine house. She could call her husband to bring his authority to bear.

I am not what I appear to be either.

Clemens walked to the gate. Their faces were only inches apart. She had the urge to reach her finger out and trace the scar on his cheek. He must have been so young when it happened.

He followed her eyes and must have seen the tenderness in them. Anger flared in his expression.

"You live here?" he asked. "All this wealth, and you chose to follow a man like Jesus?"

Wearing Tullia's luxurious veil was like putting on a different sort of armor. It made men like Clemens afraid.

"Koom," he said, glaring at her. "You cannot hide in there forever."

"There is a reason you have not seen me on the street," she replied. "I am not an agitator."

His eyes wandered up, and he looked behind her, surveying the courtyard. His eyebrows lifted. "I have never lived in a fine house. But I have dragged plenty of people out of them."

"I have committed no crime against Rome," she said.

His eyes narrowed. "I will be waiting. You and I are not done." He patted his dagger and turned back to Miriam. Shoshan had to stop him before he hurt her. But what could she do, being behind the gates, afraid to come out?

CHAPTER NINETEEN

Shoshan studied Clemens for a moment.

His mother had named him Clemens, which meant merciful. Either she had drunk too much poppy juice during delivery or she had wanted something better for her boy. Something better than a barbaric military life.

"Will you tell me her crime?" Shoshan asked.

"The neighbors have seen her out here for several nights, spying on the houses, asking who lives inside. She has taken scraps of food from the trash. She is a thief looking for a house to rob."

Miriam spoke in a rush over Clemens's words. "Antonius said you were here. I did not believe him. Why would you come here?"

"Jesus," Shoshan replied. That was as much as she dared say.

"But you should have left the city," Miriam said. "Antonius knows where you are. He is going to kill you."

Clemens snapped Miriam's arms up behind her, making her cry out. Shoshan winced, turning her face away. "Making threats against a Roman citizen is punishable by death."

Shoshan could not help her friend. Miriam was going to die in a Roman prison, all for the crime of trying to find and warn Shoshan. If Shoshan opened the gates, tried to reason with the guards or offered to go with Clemens, the plague would be discovered. Marcus and Tullia would die. And Haraka would be back on the streets.

"Miriam, please do not fight. This guard, his name is Clemens. He might yet still be merciful." Shoshan fixed him with a piercing look.

He returned her gaze with eyes that held nothing. He was a soldier, through and through.

She closed her eyes, praying. *Please, let him remember what his name means, what his mother must have wanted for him.*

"I am not unreasonable," he offered. "Do you have any information that would help me track down the last of these insurrectionists?" He looked between both women. "I will trade one life for another. Give me one of the Jesus followers. Or Jesus Himself. I have heard He is still seen on the streets by His followers. I would like to know who we really crucified, if it was not Jesus."

Of course he would assume Jesus had played a trick on everyone, either before His death or now. Clemens could not comprehend a world where death was reversed.

Shoshan looked at Miriam. Had she seen Jesus on the streets? When Miriam left Shoshan's house after the affair was discovered, when Shoshan told Miriam that Jesus had been resurrected and was seen, Miriam had left to find Him. Had she found Him?

Of course she had. That was why she was looking for Shoshan. She was willing to die to save her. Only Jesus could make a woman that brave, especially when she carried so much shame.

Shoshan and Miriam locked eyes, and everything that should have been said between them was in their gaze. Shoshan's eyes filled with tears from the sorrow of the friendship she had lost and would never have again, forgiveness for what had been done, and gratitude for what Miriam had tried to do.

Miriam's eyes misted with pain, the shame of her affair like a heavy presence between them, far thicker than the bars of iron that separated them.

Shoshan smiled, reached through the gate, and rested a tender hand on Miriam's cheek.

Miriam nestled her cheek against Shoshan's palm. A few weeks ago, Miriam had been her closest friend. They had both been happy, Shoshan thought, and looking forward to the birth of Shoshan's baby. How had they come to this?

Clemens shoved Shoshan's hand away. "Where is the man claiming to be Jesus?" he demanded. "Help me find Him, and I will let this woman go. I will never bother either of you again. A life for a life."

"Stay strong," Shoshan urged Miriam. "If Antonius promises to save you, do not trust him. I knew he was here. I caught him spying outside the gates. Remember: if he killed once, he can kill again."

From over her shoulder, she heard Haraka's sharp inhalation of surprise. She had not told Haraka about a murderer spying on them. Haraka did not even know the name Antonius.

"But he said it is already arranged. You are going to be arrested and tried for murder," Miriam said, "and then he and I will be together forever. He said Marcus's house has been looted, and that Marcus and his family are dead. You did it. He heard the details from a servant who worked for another family."

"None of that is true," Shoshan replied, sweat dotting her hairline. "I promise."

She could not reveal that Marcus was alive, though, not without jeopardizing Tullia and the baby. Clemens would know the Roman plague when he saw it. The quarantine would be called before the guards finished entering the gates.

"You are a witness," Shoshan reminded Miriam. "You know the truth, all that Antonius did. You are a liability to him."

"What we did," Miriam whispered. "It was not only him. Even then, I knew what he was capable of, Shoshan. I knew, but I did nothing to stop him. I wanted to be with him more than I wanted you to live."

The confession was a slap that shook Shoshan to her core.

She could not move. As she stepped back from the gate, she could not tear her eyes away from Miriam's face. How could Miriam have loved Antonius, knowing he wanted to kill Shoshan?

How could Jesus have sent her here, to these people? No one here deserved forgiveness.

"I will add attempted murder to your charges," Clemens announced, as happy as a child who has found an unexpected treat.

Miriam ignored him, focusing on Shoshan. "Antonius has been telling everyone there is a madwoman roaming the streets, claiming to be his dead wife. He went to Pilate this morning to make an appeal for her immediate arrest. He said that when the guards arrive, they will find Marcus and his family dead, and the house looted. You will be run through with a spear before you even hear the formal charges!"

Clemens suddenly snapped to alert.

He grabbed Miriam by the neck, twisting her to face him. "Are Pilate's men on the way here now?"

"Yes," Miriam replied weakly, tears streaming from her eyes. "I am so sorry, Shoshan."

"I do not have time for foolish pranks, and neither does Pilate." Marcus's voice startled Shoshan from her daze. "Who reported me dead?"

She twisted around to see Marcus standing on the stairs, addressing everyone as if he were the ruler of the land. *Authority has its advantages.* He knew how to take control in volatile moments. Relief flooded her body, even as panic surged back in. Marcus did not have the strength to last long.

"This woman has been troubling people in the street, sir, looking for your house." Clemens stood straight, addressing Marcus with deference. "She tells an incredible story."

He must have heard of Marcus, how important he was to the local Roman government. Marcus was the wealthiest man in this section of the city. Only now did Clemens realize this was Marcus's house, and the scandal he was caught up in.

"Yes, a grim tale. Apparently, I am dead and my house stands looted," Marcus replied, his voice cold with detached amusement. He sighed dramatically, as if for effect.

"Pilate will be furious when he learns his men were sent on a fool's errand." Marcus's voice rang through the courtyard. "He has been embarrassed enough recently, would you not agree? He was pressured into an execution that turned into a city-wide hoax."

Shoshan looked up and saw Marcus's knuckles turn white as they gripped the stair wall. He was near collapse. Saving her, saving them all, was taking every ounce of strength he had.

Clemens kicked Miriam in the back of the knees, and she fell to the ground.

"I am sorry she has disturbed you, sir," Clemens replied. He said something to the guards behind him, and they dragged Miriam away from the gate. "I will personally intercept Pilate's men and report to my commanding officer. No one else will bother you. You have my word."

"If so, I will commend you to your captain." Marcus gave a curt nod.

With that, he turned to go back upstairs, dismissing them. Shoshan saw how his thin legs trembled pitifully under his tunic. She would probably find him collapsed just inside the door.

"Shoshan!" Miriam called. "Please believe me. Antonius will not let you live!"

The plaintive echo in the street was the last Shoshan heard of Miriam's voice.

She knew she'd never see her friend again. Miriam had betrayed her. But she'd tried to warn her about Antonius. Maybe, if Shoshan searched her memories, she would see that Miriam tried to warn her about Antonius before she married him. Why had she not listened to her friend?

But Antonius had a charm that wore away at people. Relentless, cold charm that wore people down. Why had Shoshan ever thought that was a romantic quality? She shuddered to think of it now. *He wore me down. He did not win me over. I knew the difference. Why did I not listen to my conscience?*

It had to have been because of what happened in Rome so long ago. She had never felt worthy of a good man. She had only been grateful someone, anyone, wanted her.

As she turned away from the gate, she caught sight of Haraka. The effect of Miriam's arrest on the boy was palpable. He had watched Miriam roughed up by the guards then dragged away. Was he picturing his mother suffering the same fate? When he looked at Shoshan again, his eyes changed. It was as if he were seeing her for the first time, and now he distrusted her. Shoshan had watched her friend suffer and had done nothing. But she could not have saved Miriam, not without sacrificing everyone else.

"Haraka, I can explain," she began. "That woman—"

He stormed past her up the stairs. "We have to tend to your brother."

CHAPTER TWENTY

It was the next day before Marcus had the strength to speak again. Haraka spent the time in the kitchen, preparing flatbread, broth, and milk, setting trays aside for Shoshan to carry up. Whenever she entered the kitchen, he abruptly turned away.

After the noon meal, Shoshan was dipping a linen in fresh water, washing Tullia's face and body, ruminating over what had happened.

Maybe I could have done something. If I were as fast and clever as Haraka, I might have thought of a ruse to save her.

That was a painful truth, and it nagged at her. Miriam might have been saved if Shoshan had been quicker to think of something. Miriam was the deceitful one, though. Shoshan's mind did not work that way. It had never felt like a failing until now.

After dipping the linen back into the water bowl, Shoshan wrung it out, watching the water drip back into the bowl, less and less each time she squeezed. The action helped clear her mind and focus her thoughts. She plunged the linen back into the bowl, letting it absorb the water again, soaking it in, becoming heavy in her hand. She lifted Tullia's arm and washed.

Marcus would want to know why she did not warn him earlier about Antonius. What would she say? She could not bring herself to admit the failure of her marriage, not after Marcus had disowned her. It stung too much. And to tell him about the death of her daughter, how it occurred, and what Antonius did next? That wound was too raw, too painful to expose to his cold analysis.

"Who is Antonius?" Haraka demanded, interrupting her worrying. "Who did he kill?"

Shoshan whipped around, adrenaline like a bolt through her body. She did not realize he had come up the stairs behind her. Placing the linen back in the bowl, she willed her hands to stop shaking.

"Antonius killed someone?" Marcus struggled to sit up in bed. "Is that why you came here? You are hiding from the law?"

"No," Shoshan countered. "Yes, I am. But not for that reason." She turned to Haraka. "Antonius is, or was, my husband."

Haraka's eyes blazed. "You are in danger. We all are."

"Who did he kill?" Marcus demanded, his voice a thin wheeze.

"Me." Shoshan looked from Haraka to Marcus. "He killed me."

They looked back at her, uncomprehending, not even blinking. They thought she was a madwoman. The rumors Antonius had spread in the streets had an air of truth to them.

"Marcus?" Tullia said, her voice light as air. Everyone whipped their heads to look at her.

"What is happening?" Tullia asked, her eyes wide with panic. She glanced around the room as if not remembering how she had come to be here.

Shoshan rushed to Tullia's side.

"Shh, now," Shoshan murmured. "Everything is fine. You have a fever, but you are recovering." She had no idea if that was true or not. Hallucinations were common with this disease.

Thank God the servants had stolen Tullia's mirror. She did not need to know how pale and gaunt her face had become, or that her hair was starting to fall out.

"Oh," Tullia said, the word floating down like a dropped petal.

"Would you like me to rub oil on your shoulders and arms?" Shoshan asked. "That always makes me feel better and helps me sleep too."

Tullia murmured. Shoshan could not understand the words she tried to string together, and Tullia's gaze wandered. She stared at something on the ceiling, murmuring in hushed tones.

Shoshan pressed the back of her hand to Tullia's forehead. Her skin burned. Frowning, she looked at Marcus and saw his Adam's apple bob as he swallowed.

Shoshan ran to the stairs and called to Haraka, asking him to find more of the plant he had boiled the first week.

"We are desperate," she called. Turning back, she sat with Tullia, stroking her arms, waiting with her until she fell asleep. Only then did Shoshan face Marcus.

His eyes blazed when he looked at her, as if she had brought all this misfortune to his house. She had nothing to do with the plague, but he was right about the guards and Antonius.

"I wanted to tell you everything when I arrived," she said. About Antonius, Miriam, her daughter, Jesus, the resurrections… It had all been too much, even for her back then. In his weakened state it would have overwhelmed him.

"You could have left the city," he replied, despair spreading on his face. "But you came here, knowing this would ruin me."

That was exactly how the situation looked. He was harboring a known criminal, or an associate of known criminals, at the very least. Even if he survived, he realized now that his reputation would not.

"I tried to run," she replied sharply. "But Jesus, the very one you rejected, told me to come here. I did not know what I would find, but He surely did. If it were not for Him, you and Tullia would be dead."

Haraka appeared in the doorway. "I cannot go back to the market. And now I know Antonius is waiting for a chance to kill you, so you cannot go."

Shoshan whipped around to face Haraka. Was he not still furious with her?

"We will figure something out." Facing everyone now, and facing the truth, her head was swollen and heavy, and her body felt as if it were made of mud, cold and unyielding. When did she sleep last, a full night's sleep? She could not remember. Her body and mind were exhausted.

"Why can you not go to the market?" she asked.

"Because you will be alone." Haraka stared at the floor, his face dark with rage and grief.

He had to protect her because he could not protect his mother.

She could not save him from the nightmare he carried in his memories. And Tullia was declining sharply, for no reason Shoshan could guess at, other than that was just the nature of this disease. Marcus did not believe a word she said, as usual. He recognized no savior except money. But money had no power here.

A raven landed on the windowsill, its voice a harsh, scolding rasp that interrupted her thoughts.

Haraka immediately looked up at it, and she watched as his face brightened. Did he remember her words in the courtyard?

Nothing escapes His attention. He even takes care of the birds.

Shoshan drew a deep breath. She had to remember what Jesus said. Focus on His words, not her fears.

"If you have the strength," she said to Marcus, "I will tell you my story. All of it."

Haraka folded his arms, one eyebrow raised.

She smiled tenderly at him, his fierce will growing so rapidly, outpacing his body. He would become a formidable man someday.

"You too, Haraka, of course," she said. "You have earned the right to know everything. But Haraka, you are in danger if you stay. I cannot guarantee your safety."

"I do not want to be safe," he declared. "I want to make things right."

"A difficult task," she replied. "One best left to God." Haraka, set on avenging his mother and protecting Shoshan too. He had to let go of this burden.

Slowly, carefully, she explained how she began following Jesus. For Haraka's benefit, she explained how Marcus had disowned her because of the political and religious tensions around Jesus's ministry.

Marcus showed no emotion as she explained that.

She told how she had been pregnant, expecting her first child, and how she and Miriam went to the market shopping for linens for the baby, a basket to put the baby in, dried grains to boil for Shoshan for the first few weeks after delivery.

Shoshan told of her delivery, what she remembered, and what she pieced together later. That Antonius had smothered her after their daughter did not survive the birth. She did not know if he had planned that or had seen an opportunity to take advantage of her heartbreak. It was a plausible story for him to tell the authorities later. A mother who died in childbirth was common enough, but if a child did not survive, it made it even more likely the mother would not. It made it less likely that the authorities would ask questions.

She told of waking up in her grave, hearing Jesus's voice, how she waited for Him to tell her to come out. How she wandered the city, not understanding, thinking she had been in a dream, then arriving home to find Miriam in her bed. The betrayal was brutal. Miriam and Antonius thought she was a ghost looking for her daughter.

"Why was your baby not resurrected?" Haraka asked. Of course, he would have the most interest in who was resurrected, and why. He wanted every chance to see his mother again, in this life or the next.

"I do not know. But I know where my daughter is," Shoshan said. She told them of the other world, what they called heaven. There were no words she could find for it. A strange barrier existed between the worlds, even in language. *That world rebukes this one, in every way. It refuses to even be subject to our language.*

No one spoke, and it seemed to her that Marcus breathed easier as she spoke of heaven. It gave him courage to think all would not be lost, even if this disease won.

"I am glad my daughter is not here, but I wish we were not separated." Shoshan finished her story of heaven, speaking as plainly as she could.

Marcus looked away from her, toward the window.

"I do not know why some people were resurrected and brought back to Jerusalem," she added. "But all who were raised, we will all die again. We are not going to live forever here on earth."

"Why?" Marcus asked. "If Jesus died and was resurrected, why would He bring others back too? Especially if you are only going to die again. That seems cruel."

"It is all a mystery, this second life. I have accepted that now," she replied. She looked at each of them. "We are His mysteries, all of us."

A silence fell between them as each considered her words. Shoshan glanced up at the window. The raven had departed long ago in search of food or better company. Twilight had crept over Jerusalem. She caught a glimpse of the moon out of the corner of the window, a pale wash of light that softened the hard edges of the city.

The air in the room felt cleansed. Her secrets were out. She had not intended to hide any of them and had only wanted to protect everyone here, but nothing ever thrived if it was buried. There was only rot or resurrection…two extreme opposites.

Marcus had drifted to sleep as she watched the moon hovering over Jerusalem. Haraka yawned.

"Let us fix you a proper bed," she said, walking just past him to the stairs.

"If it is all right, I would like to sleep on the roof," he said.

She paused and glanced back at the window. On the roof, they'd have a view of the street below, plus the courtyard, and be able to hear if Marcus or Tullia called for help. And the moon beckoned, like a silver ball hung in the sky just for them.

"I think I will join you." She rested a hand on his shoulder. He did not flinch or pull away, and she felt a glimmer of hope. If Haraka trusted her, maybe the worst was behind them.

CHAPTER TWENTY-ONE

Marcus sat up in bed, drinking his broth. Shoshan set a cup of wine next to him on the bedside table and turned to begin washing Tullia. Her sister-in-law required all the care of a newborn. Shoshan closed her eyes, waiting for the sharp lance of pain in her heart to subside. *I will be with my daughter again someday. Just not today.*

Haraka ran down the stairs to fetch new linens for Tullia's bed. Whatever he needed to do, especially if he needed to go to market, it had to be done early today. It was Friday, and Sabbath would fall that evening.

Tullia's linens were soaked through with sweat, and there was not enough time to wash and dry them. Tullia never left the bed. Shoshan suspected Haraka would need to buy new linens at market, because there were no linens left anywhere else in the house.

"Does he ever walk?" Marcus grumbled, watching Haraka's exit from the room.

Shoshan chuckled.

"Why must he run like the building is on fire?" Marcus continued.

It was a good sign, perhaps, that Marcus was becoming more and more of his usual self, that commanding and irritable older brother.

"He is my servant and must conduct himself as such," Marcus added.

Shoshan faced him. "He is a gift from God, and you should treat him as such."

Marcus lowered his eyebrows. "Why him?" he asked. "You could have brought anyone. Why bring a child?"

Shoshan threw her hands in the air. "Do you think I picked him? That I had any choice? Of course, I would have chosen a different servant. A big, strong man. A man who looked like he belonged in a house like this."

Too late, her eyes lifted to see Haraka standing in the doorway. His chin trembled, and he dropped the linens at his feet before running.

"Haraka! Wait!" she called. "You misunderstood me!"

But he was gone, already down into the courtyard and out the gate before she was halfway down the stairs. Sitting on a step, she hung her head in her hands. How much had he heard? Probably only enough to think she did not want him. But she very much did. And she needed him.

She went to the gate and caught sight of a guard patrolling the street. Her heart raced as she ducked and pulled away from the gate. There was no way to chase after Haraka.

A servant from a neighboring house walked by, and Shoshan watched her, envious. The servant did not live in fear. *What would I give for that life?*

Thoughts of Jesus flooded her mind. She had been graced with a second life, but she no longer wanted it. If only she could talk to Him!

I do not have to live in fear. I must remember His words.

But she needed to know if Tullia and the baby would survive. She wanted to know what was going to happen, if all her efforts would be in vain, and He had said nothing about that. Also now, without Haraka, she would have to go to the market herself before the Sabbath fell. The image of Clemens patting his dagger was never far from her mind. Maybe she had ruined the plan Jesus had in mind when He sent her here. She crept back to the gate, her eyes sweeping the street in all directions. Clemens was out there, waiting.

Shoshan looked back at the stairs, and her body felt too exhausted to climb them, even one more time. She could not do this alone. It hurt to know that Jesus was out there in the city, even right now perhaps, and yet He did not help her.

A servant girl exited a house across the street, softly closing the gates behind her. She carried an embroidered robe over her arm with tears along the bottom. She was probably on her way to a seamstress. It was just an ordinary day for her.

A twinge of jealousy pinched at Shoshan.

"You there," Shoshan called softly. The servant girl stopped, looking for whoever had called for her.

Shoshan stuck her hand through the gate, waving her over. "Can I talk to you?"

The servant walked closer, frowning in confusion. Shoshan knew the situation looked odd. She appeared to be a wealthy man's wife, hiding behind the gates, calling out to another family's servant. But nothing was as it appeared. How she wished she could tell this girl the truth.

"What is the news of Jerusalem?" Shoshan said, trying to keep her voice as quiet as possible. The guard could be anywhere.

"Oh." The girl brightened, as if relieved that gossip was all this woman wanted. "Not much, really. It has been quiet since Passover."

"And Jesus?" Shoshan prompted.

The girl wrinkled her nose. "He was crucified. About three weeks ago now, I think. My mistress says it is just as well, because everyone at the temple had been in an uproar about Him. You know how she hates unrest of any kind."

"Of course," Shoshan replied, although she had never met the woman. How frustrating that this girl did not know anything recent, and probably nothing of value. No one in her house knew Jesus. They had heard of Him, but that was not the same thing. Still, Shoshan was desperate to find out where He might be.

"Is there anything else?" the girl asked, glancing down at the robe to be mended, anxious to be on her way. "My mistress will not want me to linger. An elderly man has been wandering this area, begging for leftover food. She does not like being forced into charity. That is what the temple funds are for."

"Of course," Shoshan replied. "Just one more question. Has anyone seen Jesus in these streets, or near our houses, since He was crucified?" Shoshan asked, knowing it sounded strange, but she could not stop herself.

The girl laughed, then cocked her head when she realized Shoshan was serious. "Of course not. He is dead."

"And His disciples?" Shoshan asked. "Where are they right now? Is there any gossip about them?"

"Ugh," the girl grunted. "Those men? A few are still in the city, but the guards are keeping a close eye on them. Some of them went back to fishing. A friend of mine told me that Jesus's disciples have a new rumor they are trying to spread. They say Jesus is alive, only now He can walk through walls and locked doors and appear to His disciples wherever they are. They refuse to admit the movement is over, and Jesus is not going to be crowned king."

Shoshan exhaled forcefully. Jesus was appearing to His followers even now, but He had not come to her. Why not her? She needed Him more than ever!

The servant girl walked closer to the gates. "Are you feeling well? My mistress says this house has been far too quiet lately. She was thinking of asking her husband to come over and see if everyone was all right."

"Everyone here is fine," Shoshan replied stiffly, wrapping Tullia's veil around her shoulders at an angle to drape across her face. Hopefully the girl would make the same mistake everyone else did, and assume she was Tullia.

Shoshan peeked at her, watching her face. If she had ever seen Tullia up close, this would not work.

The servant dropped her gaze immediately. "Forgive me. I only wanted to be sure you were all right. My mistress worries. She does not like anything out of place. She will be furious with me if she learns that we talked but I did not ask about your well-being."

The concern in the girl's voice moved her, and Shoshan understood what it was like to try hard to please someone who could never be pleased. Shoshan wanted to cry suddenly, to drop the veil and tell this girl everything. How long had it been since she had a friend? Miriam's betrayal seared her heart all over again.

"Tell your mistress we appreciate her concern," Shoshan replied. "We will remember her when we speak to the governor. And I will certainly remember your eagerness to serve." Shoshan smiled as she thought Marcus would, a cold smile that was a dismissal.

The girl nodded and hurried along to finish her errands.

Shoshan walked to sit beside the pool. It sparkled now, thanks to Haraka's diligent attention in removing leaves and debris daily.

Tears streamed down her face, and her shoulders shook. She wept until she had no more tears, and gulped at the air like she was drowning. She stretched out beside the pool, desperate for a moment of rest after so many sleepless nights. The disease inflicted a restless insomnia on its victims, and no one understood why. Marcus and Tullia needed extra attention after the sun set.

This was the time to remember everything Jesus had taught her, when death was all around her and discouragement was a constant temptation. Jesus was Lord, the Son of God, even in this dark place. The peace He promised to give, and the abundant life, could be true, right now, right here.

And it can be mine.

Her eyes slipped closed.

She did not know how long she slept, only that the shofar blast from the temple woke her.

The markets were closing for Sabbath. She had slept through her only chance to buy more medicine and supplies, and Haraka had not returned. When darkness fell in a few hours, she would be utterly alone, with Marcus and Tullia's lives in her hands.

Once more, twilight crept across Jerusalem, softening the glare of the sun reflecting off the limestone walls. Slowly, oil lamps appeared in windows of the houses along the street, little bowls of flame that cast shadows on the street below.

Shoshan paced in the courtyard, biting her lower lip. The city gates had closed by now. Jerusalem would be still for twenty-four hours. No markets, no public events, no festivities at Herod's palace. Just families gathered round their tables, lamps burning into the night, songs floating in the night air.

If there was any more medicine out there, she could not buy it now. And if it was outside the city, it would not come in until the day after tomorrow. The delay might mean nothing, or it might be fatal. She had no way of knowing.

Haraka had not returned. She had wounded him with her careless words, but he had misunderstood her meaning, she was sure of that. Anyone would have preferred a huge, intimidating man to keep watch over the house, but Haraka was God's surprising provision. Haraka was more than enough.

If only she had told him that. Why had she not? Now she regretted every lost opportunity to praise him and tell him that he was God's blessing to her. Now she wondered if she would have been a bad mother. It hurt to fail at loving someone who was so tenderhearted.

The creaking of the gates startled her. Haraka had opened one side of the gate and stood staring at her.

"I went to the graveyard you said you were buried in," he said. "I could find no proof of any resurrection. Every stone is in place."

"I am sure the Romans cleaned and repaired the area immediately," she replied. "They do not want anyone to know what happened. Can you imagine the danger to the empire if people realized they had crucified the Son of God? That the Messiah had walked among us and they killed Him?"

"Were you really dead?" he asked, his chin tilted up. He looked defiant.

"Yes." She wanted to run across the courtyard and hug him, but she had wounded him too badly. He was still angry.

"And Jesus?" Haraka demanded.

"He is who He said He is," she replied. "He is God walking among us. And He is the one who gave me life again."

"Do you think He could do that for my mother?" His voice was so soft she might have missed it. Haraka refused to meet her gaze as he said the words.

His words seared her heart. He did not know where his mother was, or if she was still living. He wanted a promise from Shoshan that she could not give.

"I know you want to see her again," Shoshan said as gently as she could.

A tear trickled down his cheek. Turning, he rested his forehead against the gate.

She took a step forward. "He is a God of many miracles, Haraka. I did not know your mother, and I do not know everything about this second life that Jesus offers, but I do know that God never runs out of miracles. We could pray together, you and I, that He would do one for your mother."

"But she might be—" He could not finish the sentence.

"God is an eternal God, Haraka. I do not think He sees death like we do. He will not reject your prayer just because you do not know her circumstances. He knows your heart."

She walked to him and pulled him inside the gate. "Come back inside, Haraka. This is your home now." She shut the gate behind him.

He stood, arms hanging at his sides, a broken boy, and then before she could blink, his arms were wrapped tightly around her, and he wept.

With one hand, she stroked his hair as she held onto him.

"It is all right, Haraka," she whispered. "Everything is going to be all right. We are two little sparrows, you and I."

"And He takes care of the birds," Haraka said between shuddering breaths.

"Mistress?" an unfamiliar voice called out.

Together, Haraka and Shoshan looked in the direction of the gate. An elderly man stood there, his clothes in tatters, his beard longer than any beard she'd ever seen. Except for…

"Oh!" Shoshan went to the gate, opening it at once. "You are the man buried in the vegetable patch!"

A slight frown passed over his face before his eyes lit in sudden recognition. "And you are the woman who joined us in the codex shop. You were late, as I remember."

"I was trying to evade the guards," Shoshan said. She wanted to embrace him, but he was still frail-looking. "How are you? Do you have a home? Can I help you?"

Her questions tumbled out too quickly. He reached to rest a trembling hand on her arm, as if to slow her down. "I need no home.

Besides, I think this old body will not last much longer. While I am here, though, I am working with all my strength, as little as it may be. What about you, my dear friend?"

"I am working hard too," she confessed. Turning, she pointed to Haraka. "I have help, though. Are you sure you do not need anything?"

"But I do, yes," the man replied. "Do you have any food? Anything at all, or money? I can use money."

Was he hungry? Was he the beggar her neighbors were trying to avoid? He must have read the questions on her face. "It is not for me. I will not live long enough to enjoy money, anyway. But I was shocked to learn how expensive everything is, and that the temple is failing the people. The Sanhedrin are taxing the widows and then driving them from their homes for lack of payment. All that money paid into the temple treasury, and so few coins land in the hands of widows? It breaks my heart to hear of it. I am determined to feed the widows and find shelter for them. It is hard work, and I do not like begging, but it is better for me to do it than them. I have no pride or reputation left to protect."

Haraka ran into the kitchen and returned quickly with a loaf of bread and several coins left from his last trip to market. Shoshan did not know how much money remained upstairs, but surely this man needed whatever they could give.

The man's eyes glistened with tears as he accepted the gift from Haraka. Resting a hand on the boy's head, he blessed him in the old tradition.

"God bless you and keep you, my son, the Lord make His face to shine upon you, and be gracious to you. The Lord lift up His countenance upon you, and give you peace."

Haraka stood so still it was as if he did not dare to breathe. The words seemed to fill him, to reach his heart in a way nothing had before.

As the man turned and left, Shoshan understood. Haraka had never known a father's love, much less a blessing from the hand of one.

Suddenly she felt very sorry for anyone who had turned this man away. They had missed sharing in a blessing, in more ways than one.

CHAPTER TWENTY-TWO

That night, Shoshan and Haraka sat on the roof, waiting for the dawn. Both had trouble sleeping through the night now that their sleep was so often interrupted. Every so often, one of them would go below to check on Tullia and Marcus. Both slept, thank God. Shoshan apologized to Haraka and explained what he had overheard and what her true meaning had been. It was not an easy conversation, and he resisted her attempts to pat his arm as she talked, but he did not run away again. He seemed to accept her explanation. God's provision to her by sending Haraka had been a thousand times better than what she might have chosen. It was one of the reasons she was sure he was a gift from God.

Haraka liked the idea of being chosen by the God of the universe.

Shoshan lay down, hoping to close her eyes for a few minutes before the sunrise. The Sabbath day would not be a day of rest for her, not with two deathly ill patients to care for.

Haraka went below to check on Marcus and Tullia one last time before sleep.

In a flash, he bounded back up the ladder, his eyes wide with fear.

"I cannot wake Tullia," he cried.

Shoshan hurried down the ladder with him at her heels. The bedroom was heavy with the scent of perspiration and a different, acrid smell, one unique to this disease. Shoshan wished for more air, but the window was not wide enough to give circulation.

Shoshan turned to look at Haraka and put a finger to her lips, warning him not to wake Marcus. Moonlight flooded across the floor at an angle, and she crossed the beam, dread slowing her footsteps. Tullia's bed was just outside the beam of glowing light.

Was she dead? The baby too?

Her hand shook as she reached for Tullia. *Please, do not let her be dead.*

Shoshan rested her hand on Tullia's chest. It did not feel warm, but it was not cold either, not like a corpse. Pressing more firmly, Shoshan closed her eyes, concentrating. The faintest whisper of breath stirred in Tullia's lungs. Moving her hand to the belly, Shoshan pressed down but felt no movement. The baby might be sleeping though. There might be hope, even now.

"She is alive," Shoshan whispered. "Barely." Turning, she gestured toward the stairs. Haraka shook his head slowly from side to side and went to the wall above Marcus's bed. Carefully, silently, he slipped the stone from its place and grabbed a handful of coins.

Shoshan bit her lip. She could not argue or ask what he was doing, not here, not without the risk of waking Marcus up. If Marcus woke now and realized how close to death Tullia and the baby were, he would panic. He would call for the guards himself.

Shoshan jabbed her finger at the stairs. Haraka was already out of the room and down the stairs before she had descended the first three steps to follow.

In the courtyard, he slipped the coins into the tiny bag on his belt.

"What are you doing?" she asked, keeping her voice low. "Everything is closed. Everyone is inside with their doors locked. It is the Sabbath."

"I have to find the man who sold you the plant," Haraka said. "I think I know where he lives."

"It is too dangerous!" she argued. "The streets are too quiet. You will be spotted."

Haraka scowled. "It does not matter. No one can catch me."

"The guards will see you come back here, and they will stop you," she replied. "You will not be able to explain yourself, not without giving us away. Even the letter Marcus signed will not get you out of trouble now."

"You worry too much," he said, then added one thing. "I have to try. This is my home now. You said so yourself."

Shoshan ran her hands through her hair, scared and frustrated. "I know I did. But Antonius wants to hurt me, and if he has seen you…"

"I bought a dagger today," Haraka said, lifting his shirt to reveal a glittering knife that was as long as his forearm.

"Haraka, no. I do not want you carrying a weapon." This was spiraling out of her control.

"I am going to kill a man someday anyway. I made an oath."

"You can rescind an oath," she said.

"You are not my mother!" he shot back.

"It is because of your mother that I say this: Revenge will ruin you, Haraka. God has another plan for you. Please do not do this. Take the dagger off. Stay here. We will figure this out together."

"How do you know what plans God has for me?" Haraka asked, his voice rising in pitch and volume. "You do not even know what His plan is for you! I hear you praying in the courtyard when you think we are all asleep. You are scared."

She lowered her voice, hoping he would do the same. "Of course I am scared. I do not know what to do, you are right. I do not know what the Lord's plan is. I only know that I am supposed to be here, and there is work to be done."

The sound of Marcus clearing his throat interrupted them. Both whipped around to look at him standing on the stairs, pale as a ghost, his eyes vacant.

"Tullia is dead," he announced. Then he sank down, slowly, as if the last of his strength had left him too. He sat on the stairs, dazed, staring into the darkness.

Shoshan and Haraka locked eyes. Shoshan ran for the stairs to check on Tullia, praying Marcus was wrong. Tullia's pulse and breathing were so feather-light, surely he had missed it.

"Go," Shoshan urged Haraka. "Bring whatever help you can find, medicine or healer."

Haraka ran for the gates and disappeared into the night. Shoshan said a quick prayer for him as he flew down the street and into the silence of the city. A faint tinge of pink was visible to the east. Dawn approached. Haraka would not be able to move safely in the shadows. He would be exposed for anyone to see as he ran. Never before had she feared the dawn like she did at this moment.

If they all survived this Sabbath, it would be a miracle.

Shoshan raced across the bedroom floor to check on Tullia, brushing past Marcus, who sat expressionless on the stairs. He looked near death himself from the shock of waking and finding Tullia like that.

Shoshan pressed her hand once more against Tullia's chest. *Nothing.* Pressing harder, Shoshan strained to detect life. Still, she could feel nothing. Quickly, she grabbed a linen from the water bowl and wet her own cheek then pressed it near Tullia's face. Hovering there, Shoshan heard her own heart pounding in her ears. *Please.* A faint whisper of breath across her wet cheek made her gasp in relief. *Thank You, Lord.*

As if aware of Shoshan's presence, Tullia drew in a deeper breath, her chest rising and falling almost imperceptibly, bringing tears to Shoshan's eyes. Glancing at Tullia's belly, she knew she had to try and check for life there too. Was the baby still alive? Her knees went weak at the thought of losing the baby. She could not face another death like that, one of a babe who never even opened its eyes on this world.

"What do we do now?" Marcus leaned against the doorway. His voice was that of a child, a child who was lost and afraid.

"Tullia is alive," Shoshan said over her shoulder, still trying to find any sign of life in the womb. "Haraka has gone to get medicine."

Finally, Shoshan stood. She had not been able to find any signs of life. But that did not mean the baby was gone. She had to avoid meeting Marcus's eyes though, for fear of what he might read in hers.

"The baby is due in about three weeks, more or less," Shoshan said to herself, calculating the time passed since she had arrived. Tullia was not a reliable source for her exact due date, not with the fever affecting her mind. Still, Shoshan tried to be hopeful. Some babies came early, some came late. Many survived against the odds. As long as there was life, there was hope. But she had no way of knowing if the baby was still alive, not unless the baby moved while she was pressing against Tullia's stomach.

"Do you have a midwife picked out?" Shoshan asked, focusing now on Marcus. A midwife would know whether the baby was still living and, if the baby was still alive, when to expect Tullia's labor pains to begin.

He blinked, still trying to come back from the terror of thinking Tullia was gone. He managed to nod and shared the name of the midwife.

He was scared. For the first time in his life, he might lose, and he knew it. His fate, and hers, was completely out of his control.

Shoshan knew that if Marcus was healthy and in control, he'd have the best physicians and midwives there already. Tullia would have the best care in the empire at her bedside, instead of Shoshan and the street orphan Haraka.

Shoshan looked at the stairs, willing Haraka to materialize again, medicine in hand.

Marcus stared at Tullia, and his features were twisted again with grief. He was probably thinking of how little he could do, she realized. All his life he had pursued money and power, but here, when it mattered most, he was helpless. He had no power against this enemy, and money could only buy things. If money could save Tullia, she would have recovered long before this.

"I worked hard to get where I am. I thought I was doing it for us," he said. He must have been thinking many similar things, staring at a pregnant wife he could not save. "But I turned my back on you. You must hate me."

"I know how hard you worked," Shoshan replied gently. "I never resented you for that."

"But why Jesus?" Marcus lifted his head, catching her eye from over his shoulder. "He had no money. No influence. You wanted to follow Him, even though you knew I would be forced to disown you. You loved Jesus more than your own brother."

He sounded wounded. Shoshan fought the urge to argue, even as the offense she felt grew. He thought he was the injured one? Even now, he did not see what she had been through with Antonius. And he did not understand what she was enduring to save his wife. Every touch, every act of tender care, was a reminder of the baby she had lost.

"Do you know the real reason why our family left Rome?" Shoshan asked. "What happened to me?"

Marcus's body stiffened. He must have known. Or at least, he had a very good idea.

"You left me alone at the library of scrolls," she said. "It was the day you wanted to sneak away and buy sweets with the money you had saved. You told me I was not allowed to follow you. You said I had to find my own way home."

Marcus nodded, and then his body became still.

That day, Shoshan had sat on the steps of the library for what felt like hours. She did not know how to get home. Her older brother Marcus had always held her hand and led her home, keeping her safe. But that day was the first day he'd had money, and he did not want to be weighed down by a younger sister.

"I was only six," Shoshan said, the words sticking in her throat. Her throat burned with the tears she forced back.

Marcus exhaled, hanging his head.

That day, she had spied an older boy, well-dressed, luring an old man into a shadowed doorway. Hiding, Shoshan had watched helplessly as the boy viciously struck the man on the head and stole his money bag. She had never witnessed violence before this moment. Marcus had protected her all her life. When the boy ran off with his stolen prize, Shoshan ran to check on the old man and could not find any signs of life. She ran to the guards next, weeping as she told them what she had seen, and gave a perfectly accurate description of the attacker.

The guards brought her home and warned her mother and father to keep Shoshan silent or leave Rome immediately. Shoshan's description of the attacker matched one of the sons of a powerful Roman senator, a young man well-known to the guards for his thievery and violence. Her parents could not report the crime—the senator would never allow that. Besides, the guards pointed out, Shoshan's parents were Hebrews, anyway, and there had been a recent uprising among the Jews in the eastern provinces over taxes. No one wanted to hear their troubles.

Every time she remembered the attack, she wondered if she could have done something different, something that might have spared the old man. Marcus had withdrawn from her after that, and it broke her heart. Now she knew he probably felt the same guilt she did, of not being able to save the man, plus the guilt of leaving her alone that day. She had watched her mother's trembling chin as the house was shuttered and their belongings packed, and noted her father's grim silence. Shoshan knew she was at the center of the tragedy, and somehow that felt the same as if she had caused it.

"I was so stupid to leave you alone in the streets," Marcus said, his voice barely audible. "For years after that, I tortured myself with the thought of what that boy could have done to you if he knew you witnessed the attack. You would not be alive today, I suspect."

"But that did not happen, and I thank God for it," she replied. She touched her face and was surprised to find her cheeks were wet. It had been so long since she cried over that memory, the day her childlike delight in the city was shattered. Sin had broken her heart, and she had never been able to pick up the pieces. They were scattered in a Roman street far away.

And then, in a flash of another memory, she remembered the One who did pick up broken pieces, all of them. When Jesus fed her among the crowd of five thousand men, He had insisted that the disciples pick up every broken piece that was left over.

At the time, she had not understood. Maybe, to the disciples, His request held a different meaning, but to her, now she saw the beauty of that moment. Jesus loved the broken pieces. Each one mattered to Him.

He will let nothing be wasted.

The comfort was a warm feeling, an insulation against the cold winds she walked through.

Marcus turned and embraced her. "I am so sorry, Shoshan. It is my fault, not yours, that we had to leave Rome."

For a moment, Shoshan was too surprised to move. Marcus had not embraced her since before that day so long ago. After another moment, she softened and returned his hug.

"I forgive you, Marcus. I always have. It was not your fault. It was not either of our faults."

"I hated the Romans after that," he confessed. He dropped his arms and pulled back, staring her in the face. "I hated them for not having the courage to do what was right. When my career first started, I told myself that I wanted power so I could change the government, so everyone would have justice, no matter how little money they had. But then I tasted wealth too, and look what I became. Now I do not fight for justice. Only for more power, more money."

The painful knot in her throat flared again.

"I need to ask you something. Antonius wanted money, and power too, but I never supported his ambitions the way he wanted me to. Perhaps because I cared about different things. Should I have wanted those same things? Is it my fault he betrayed me?" Shoshan asked, if only because she needed to say the words out loud.

Marcus's temper flared. His eyes blazed, and his posture stiffened to that of a man ready for a fight. This time, he was ready to fight for her, and she felt a swell of relief at the sight.

"Antonius is a fool," Marcus said. "By my word, you will never have to live with him again."

Tullia's eyes fluttered open briefly. Shoshan and Marcus both snapped to attention and rushed to comfort her. Shoshan held a cup of broth to her lips as Marcus propped her head up, urging her to drink. Marcus exchanged a look with Shoshan that said he knew how desperate they were now. There might be only hours left to save Tullia or the baby. Every drop of broth they could get Tullia to drink would give her more strength for the delivery.

Tullia sputtered, and broth dribbled down her chin. They tried again, then again, draining the jug of broth Haraka had made.

The morning sun was full and high above Jerusalem now.

Marcus looked back at the stairs, then at Shoshan. She understood. Haraka had not returned, and they needed medicine if there was any hope of saving Tullia or the baby.

Haraka was fast, but she could not shake the feeling he was trying to outrun death itself.

CHAPTER TWENTY-THREE

Hours passed without Haraka's return. Sitting beside Tullia, holding her limp hand, Shoshan knew what she had to do. She had to go and get the midwife. There was no other option. Haraka might not return. Anything could have happened to him on the street.

But if she went herself and left now, on the Sabbath and barely past noon, she would be seen on the street.

But there was another problem. She could not leave Marcus alone with Tullia. If Antonius broke in looking for Shoshan, Marcus would not have the strength to fight. Antonius could kill him, and he might consider killing Tullia too. Antonius probably assumed that if Marcus and Tullia both died, Shoshan, if alive, would inherit the estate. That was how the laws of inheritance worked among the Hebrews. He would not harm Shoshan if he realized how close she was to inheriting the estate.

Marcus must have read her thoughts.

"Go. If Antonius comes, and I die, at least a midwife will be on her way for Tullia," he said. "My life for hers. The baby might live."

Shoshan felt a twinge of pain. Antonius had never felt that kind of devotion to her. What had been going through his mind when he watched her labor with their child? Had he been planning her death even then, or had it been an impulsive decision? She would probably never know the truth. She wondered if that was better.

"Maybe Haraka will return while I am out," she said. "He went for help."

The midwife would surely recognize Marcus's address right away, so Shoshan should not have any trouble convincing her to come. Even on a Sabbath. *Babies came on the Sabbath all the time. They did not know it was a day of rest.* Shoshan remembered her own labor, those long, painful hours of struggle…

"You have to go, Shoshan," Marcus said. "One more time, for me, you will be alone on the streets and in danger. But if you believe in Jesus as you say you do, you will find your courage."

"I do," Shoshan replied. "And you are right, I have to trust Him for help."

"And if you trust in Him, you will not be truly alone out there," Marcus prompted.

He was right, of course. Was he beginning to understand who Jesus was, and what He meant to her?

Shoshan bent and kissed Tullia on the forehead. The sweat on her skin had dried, leaving a fine, salty grit, and Shoshan felt how warm her skin still was. The fever had not spiked yet this afternoon, but it simmered just beneath the surface.

Just a month ago, Marcus could have bribed or bullied his way out of any situation. Tullia was his delight, and he resisted the idea that she should ever lift a finger, even in her own house. But now Tullia was locked in mortal combat and had to fight her biggest battle without him.

"You are not fighting alone," Shoshan whispered to Tullia, pulling back and staring her in the face, willing her to hear. "Ask God to help you."

Her eyes opened, just a tiny flutter of eyelashes.

"I saw Jesus do miracles—did I tell you?" Shoshan continued, as if they were two old friends picking up a conversation they had just left off. "He can do anything, anything at all. I am going to fetch the midwife now, and when I return, you are going to have a baby."

Shoshan dipped a linen in water and wiped Tullia's forehead.

"One last drink before I go. You will need your strength." She lifted another spoonful of milk and pressed it between Tullia's lips.

"There was a blind man who Jesus healed. The man's name is Timaeus, and he is a friend of mine," Shoshan said, helping Tullia drink. "Think about what it means for you. He was born blind. Then he met Jesus." Angling the cup again, she watched as more milk disappeared into Tullia's mouth. Shoshan waited until she saw movement in Tullia's throat. *Thank God. She is drinking.*

"Timaeus was born with eyes that did not see. Jesus healed his eyes, and now Timaeus sees the world, a world that once he only knew by sound. Do you understand what I am telling you?" Shoshan gave her another drink, and Tullia accepted it. "Jesus touched eyes that never worked, never once in this life, and now Timaeus sees a world he never knew existed."

She drained the last of the milk into Tullia's mouth and waited for her to swallow.

"There is a world beyond what you know, Tullia," she whispered. "Do not be afraid. No matter what happens, Jesus can give you life."

Tullia's eyes opened farther. She was listening. Marcus leaned toward them, attentive, his breath ragged.

"I am telling you the truth," Shoshan whispered to her, urging her to take more milk. "I lost my daughter. But I know where she is, and I know she is alive."

Tullia winced.

Shoshan wiped her mouth where milk had spilled. "Jesus opened my eyes too, but in a different way. There is another world that exists. Do not be afraid. But you must fight right now. Fight for your baby, and fight for your life, but do not fight like a woman afraid of dying."

Shoshan rested a hand on Tullia's belly. "Fight like a woman who believes in miracles."

Tullia locked eyes with her then, and Shoshan knew she understood. Tullia was about to enter a fight that she had no strength to win. Her only hope would be Jesus.

Shoshan set the empty cup on the bedside table and walked downstairs.

Two men she had never seen before paced in the courtyard. They were huge men, tall and muscular, and judging by their ornate robes, definitely not Hebrews. Pressing herself against the wall, as if that would do any good, she watched them, her heart pounding, her breath stinging her lungs. They explored the courtyard, whispering to each other.

Strangers had invaded the home, and Haraka was nowhere to be seen.

Shoshan had only a moment, she knew, before they spotted her on the stairs. She strained to see any clue as to their identity. They were not wearing Roman armor. The one closest to the stairs had kohl streaked under his eyes. His eyes were wide, dark slashes that glittered as he surveyed the courtyard. When he looked up, his face was menacing, and Shoshan yelped in fright.

"Do not be afraid!" It was Haraka's voice. "They are with me."

She turned, relief flooding her body when she heard his voice. Haraka had returned. But confusion and fear replaced the feeling immediately. She did not move from her perch on the stairs, still afraid of the men, but called down to Haraka.

"Did you get the plant?" she called.

Haraka barked an order to the kohl-eyed man, who promptly lumbered toward the servants' quarters.

Slowly, she picked her way down the stairs, keeping an eye on the other stranger. Haraka ran across the courtyard, hugging her impulsively then stepping back.

"I could not get the medicine. The old man has left the city. Maybe tomorrow, when the gates reopen after the Sabbath, he will return."

"Tomorrow will be too late. We must deliver the baby today," she said, and watched as his face fell. "But thank you, Haraka. You did well. You are a marvel."

He lifted his chin, and his cheeks flushed. How long had it been since anyone had praised him the way his mother would have? He was probably starved for the words she would have said.

Shoshan explained her errand, that she had to fetch a midwife, and that Haraka must stay to guard the house.

"The baby needs to come," Haraka agreed. "Tullia will not last much longer. I have seen women that look like her. The end comes quickly."

"Do not talk like that, Haraka. She is alive, so there is much hope. I have seen miracles that defy explanation. I am one."

"You saw Jesus do those miracles," Haraka said. "But where is He now?"

"I do not know," she replied. "I just do not. And I do not understand that."

Next, Shoshan nodded to the man pacing the courtyard. The kohl-eyed man returned from the servants' quarters carrying a satchel, perhaps whatever Haraka had been able to find with the markets closed.

"Who are those men?" she said lowering her voice.

"Friends from Herod's Theater. They will patrol the courtyard and pretend to be our guards in exchange for good food." He hesitated. "You said you wanted big, strong men."

She looked at him, puzzled, then remembered. "I did say that. Although you misunderstood me, Haraka. I would not trade you for ten of them."

He grinned.

She walked to the gates, drawing a deep breath before she left, unsure if she would be safe on the streets. Maybe Jesus would come to her, find her out there and tell her what to do next. The gates creaked in protest as she cracked them open and slipped out into the deserted street.

Running down the silent streets, Shoshan felt the back of her neck prickle. She turned down one street, then another, but the feeling intensified. It was an uneasy feeling, and she knew it had nothing to do with Jesus. The farther she ran, the closer the danger seemed to be. The midwife lived in a little house nestled amid the shops, which were all closed today. The streets were still. Nothing and no one moved. But something stirred, nonetheless.

She did not dare stop and look. *It is just my imagination. I have to reach the midwife and bring her back.*

The midwife's street was just ahead, and Shoshan felt a surge of energy as she turned the corner. Just a few steps more and help would be on the way.

A blinding-fast assault slammed her against the limestone wall of the building. Her head bounced, connecting with the stone, and a warm wet spot spread across her scalp. A hand clamped around her mouth as her assailant dragged her backward into a shop. It stood empty and dark. Today was the Sabbath, a holy day of rest. Shoshan's mind was frantic, scrambling for explanations of any kind.

She was thrown to the ground and heard the door close behind her. Pushing herself to all fours, she looked up.

Antonius loomed over her.

"If I kill you nicely, will you promise to stay dead this time?" He smirked.

She crawled backward, trying to get away from him, her knees scraping on the floor. His leg shot out, and he kicked her in the side, the toe of his sandal hitting her in the stomach. She collapsed, her hand over the area. She could not breathe, although her mouth was open and she tried to inhale. When breath finally pushed through, it had a rasping sound.

He watched her the way he might have watched an insect crawling on a piece of fruit he intended to eat. He was going to kill her. But the mocking, the cruelty in his eyes, pierced her heart more than even that realization. He did not seem to care that he had kicked her in the stomach, only weeks after his child had lived there within her.

His expression told her everything. He mocked her new life, and he mocked Jesus. Even now, he refused to believe that Jesus had raised her from the dead. Either he did not think she was worthy of such a miracle, or he did not think Jesus capable of one. It did not matter now.

"Let me go, Antonius."

She stopped herself before she said anything else. She could not betray Marcus and Tullia. She did not want him to know that Tullia was pregnant, let alone close to delivery and possible death.

"Where are you running to, little rat? And on the Sabbath of all days. I thought you were a devout believer, but maybe you will bend the rules when it suits you." He made a tsking sound. "Everything all right at the estate? Anything that requires my attention?"

She pressed her lips together and refused to answer.

He shrugged. "Perhaps after I kill you, I will go and see for myself."

She lunged for his legs but he leaped out of her reach, laughing at her.

"Stay away from my brother!" she yelled, then pushed herself to stand and face him, her hands balled into fists.

He folded his arms, watching her. "I want to know how you did it. How did you fake your death?"

She tried to push past him and get out the door, but he caught her and threw her back to the ground.

"When I tracked you down, the first thing I did was to make sure Miriam found out where you were," he said, sounding smug. "I knew she would come to find you. She was telling everyone she had seen Jesus. He must have shaken her up quite badly. She wanted nothing else to do with me. But she told me how badly she wanted to apologize to you for what she had done."

"What you both did," Shoshan replied immediately.

"I never betrayed you," Antonius said, his expression one of mock outrage as he pressed his hand to his chest. "I was a devoted husband. That is the word on the street. Everyone has seen me weeping, seeking solace at the synagogue."

She recoiled. His pantomime was sickening.

"And even if I did not really love you, who is there to say otherwise?" He dropped his hand to his side and shrugged, as if the matter was closed. "There will not be any witnesses left."

"You wanted Miriam killed," Shoshan said, more to herself than him. "You set her up. Why? To cover up that your relationship started while you and I were married, or because she knows what you did to me?"

She looked at Antonius, wondering how she had ever loved him.

He was unperturbed by her accusation. Instead, he picked at something in his teeth then studied his fingertip. "It was easy to spread rumors, to get all of Marcus's neighbors on alert, and send a guard to Marcus's house to arrest her. Rich people are so nervous when there is unrest in the streets. Your neighbors think I have done them all a great favor. That I am a sad widower who only wants to see justice done. I believe they will reward me, especially if I turn in another agitator. You see, no matter how this plays out, I win. I win, and you die."

"They will see you for who you are," she replied, her disdain for him complete.

"People see what they want to see," he scoffed. "Especially when it is convenient."

"If you kill me and get a reward, what then?" Shoshan asked, morbidly curious. "A new wife? Start over in another city?"

Antonius groaned. "It is so much work to move. I would need money to make it worthwhile. Marcus is a good businessman. I will make him an offer. For a price, I will say nothing to the authorities. No one will know that he harbored a fugitive."

Antonius had not found out about the plague, clearly.

"Marcus will never bargain with you," she replied. "And there is no proof he sheltered me. He disowned me. Everyone knows that."

He shook his head, as if in regret. "And yet here you are, wearing Tullia's freshly washed clothes."

He was right. Marcus would never be able to explain that. If the plague was discovered, even if he lived, how would he explain how he survived without help? The truth about his servants looting his house and leaving him to die would come out. *Think. What is Antonius's weakness?*

"You are right," she admitted. "I have given myself away by wearing these clothes."

An idea shimmered in her mind. She licked her lips, but her mouth was dry. Would Antonius be so gullible?

"But there is one thing Marcus would want more, even more than your silence, more than your agreement to leave the city," she said.

"What is that, dear?"

Please let this work.

"Favor with Rome," she said, hoping he did not hear the fear in her voice.

"Yes? Go on." He waited.

She spoke quickly. "If he turned me in himself, he would earn favor with Rome. Imagine, a man in his position turning in his own sister. They would fall all over themselves to reward him. Pilate especially would appreciate the gesture."

"Why would I not do it myself, then, if Rome would be so appreciative?"

"And how would you explain the grave you bought for me? The funeral? You need *me* to keep my mouth shut, Antonius, not the other way around. Imagine, though, if Marcus moves up in the Roman government, becoming Caesar's right-hand advisor, and you are the one who put him there?"

She laughed lightly, hoping Antonius did not pause to think. It was a bold plan but not one she had thought through. She didn't quite believe it herself. But the rewards would be, in theory, much greater. The theory was all she had right now though.

Antonius grabbed her by the arm and yanked her to her feet.

"Let us go see your brother." He pushed her through the door and out onto the deserted street.

CHAPTER TWENTY-FOUR

"O pen the gates!" Antonius commanded.

The two strangers blocked the gates.

Helpless, Haraka watched the exchange. His hired men, who appeared so imposing, immediately looked to him for instructions.

Shoshan nodded. *Do not interfere*, she willed him.

Once the gates were open, Antonius wasted no time. Pushing Shoshan ahead of himself, he took the stairs, walked into the bedroom, and stopped abruptly. He was stunned as he looked from Marcus to Tullia and back again. The disheveled linens on the beds, the pallor of their faces, the milk and broth at each bedside. The odor of bodies, feverish and unbathed for weeks now. Sickness hung in the air.

"What is this?" Antonius murmured, staring at Tullia. He had only seen her on her wedding day, in her beautiful dress, with her hair done and cosmetics on. Now he saw a pale, thin girl with tangles all around her pillow, eyes sunken into her head, her belly swollen, the bed linens stained with drips of old broth and milk.

Marcus sat up, eyes wide as his mind worked, surveying the situation. Shoshan could see his arms twitching, as if trying to find the strength to protect Tullia.

"The plague," Shoshan replied.

She could see the facts becoming clear to Antonius. This house should have been in quarantine. Everyone in the house would die, including Shoshan, and...

"And you would have inherited the estate," Shoshan finished his thought. "But you brought me back here, hoping to blackmail my brother. You cannot afford to stay in the city now. You know too much. You must either report this and agree to be quarantined with us or flee."

"No one saw me enter the gate." Antonius looked around the room wildly, as if there was any other explanation or any way out.

"You cannot be sure of that," Shoshan replied, then pressed her point. "Now that you know our secret, you are a part of it. Leave Jerusalem. Go to another city, where you can wait until you receive the news that we are all dead. Then you can claim the estate."

"You might not all die," Antonius replied. His face changed as he spoke, and she knew his mind was leaping ahead, thinking through all of his options. "And if Marcus survives, the estate will not change hands."

"That is true," she replied, with more confidence than she felt. "But you will know that Marcus hid the plague from the authorities. I am sure Marcus will pay you for your silence."

"I will send a message to the guards right now and be done with you, once and for all," Antonius sputtered, moving toward the stairs. "No one will know who gave them the tip."

Haraka's men blocked his exit. Haraka stood at the bottom of the stairs, watching.

"You have told too many lies, Antonius," Marcus said, finally. "The city is full of people who do not trust you. No one will want to

MYSTERIES & WONDERS *of the* BIBLE

get involved with a man who claims to have seen the plague here in Jerusalem. You are the same man who claims he buried his wife, but many people can verify that Shoshan is alive."

"The authorities would have questions about that, would they not?" Shoshan added. "You have made a spectacle of yourself as a grieving widower, but I am alive. They would want to talk to the midwife you hired, the one who declared me dead. They would talk to the neighbors and find out about your affair. How suspicious that makes you look! It would not be hard for them to realize you were the one who set Miriam up to be arrested. The guards do not like being treated like fools. They would want revenge, Antonius. You would not even make it to the prison alive."

"You are welcome to stay, of course, and die with us," Marcus added, contempt in his voice. He refused to even look at Antonius, and instead looked at Shoshan, his eyebrows raised expectantly.

"I did not reach her," Shoshan told him, referring to the midwife. "Antonius stopped me before I could get to her house."

Marcus stood, his legs wobbling for a brief second before he righted himself and faced Antonius.

"You…" Marcus edged closer to him, his fury coloring his pale cheeks in a dark red. It was like watching a shadow of the man he had once been, Shoshan thought. The old anger was there, but he was so weak.

Antonius backed up, hands out, palms facing Marcus. He did not want the plague.

But was it even contagious? Shoshan had not contracted it. Haraka had not either. Was there a legitimate reason for Rome to quarantine houses with this disease?

Marcus continued to advance, and Antonius backed away. The men blocking the stairs looked at each other, panicked, wanting no part of this dispute. Without warning, they fled downstairs, leaving Antonius. Maybe they were afraid of the plague too.

Antonius had edged away until he stood with his back to the stairs, his heels balancing on the landing.

Marcus took another step then coughed on him intentionally.

Antonius screamed as he fell, tumbling down the stairs, the noise reverberating through the courtyard. He landed at the bottom, bruised and dazed, looking up in terror at Marcus. Haraka stood near him, arms pinned to his side, frozen in shock and fear.

The stairs were not high enough, or steep enough, to kill him. Shoshan peered over her brother's shoulder, unsure what to feel. She didn't want Antonius alive, not if he was a threat, but she didn't want her brother to murder him either.

Marcus took the first step down, clearly intending to finish the job. Shoshan reached out and grabbed him by the shoulder.

"No, Marcus," she urged. "Not like this."

Marcus turned and looked at her. "After all he did to you? And he stopped you from getting the midwife for Tullia! Why would you ask for mercy for him?"

"I am not," she replied, her breath whooshing out from her chest all at once. "I am asking for your sake. For your family."

Suddenly, she was so tired of all this fighting, all this anger and revenge. "Marcus, you have carried too much guilt in your life, and for too long. I cannot let you do this. It would only add to your burden."

He shook her hand off. "Eye for an eye. That is the law of Moses."

"I do not argue that. But there is a new way. A new law," she said. "Do unto others as you would have done to yourself."

"Who said that?" Marcus frowned.

Shoshan felt heat rising to her cheeks. One look from him and she felt like a child.

He studied her, then shook his head. He looked down at Antonius, who had begun to crawl to safety, then back at his sister, a twitch appearing at the sides of his mouth. "You are quoting Jesus, are you not? You are trying to convert me, right in the middle of me killing a man. You never know when to quit, do you?"

She pressed her lips together, feeling like a child, but refusing to argue. She was right, and he knew it, but he was too stubborn to agree with her, just like when they had been children together. He had never wanted to stop before he had his full measure, even back then.

"You are going to be a father," she said. "You have to think about your legacy."

His mouth pulled down at the edges, but he cleared his throat and pushed past her into the bedroom.

Below, Antonius stood and looked up at her. He wiped his nose with the back of his hand, and she saw a tinge of blood.

"Why did I ever love you?" she asked thoughtfully as she considered her own question, thinking back, trying to find justification for her decision to marry him. "Tell me honestly, if you can. How did you do it?"

"Do what?" he asked, sullen, rubbing one shoulder.

"Convince Miriam, and me, that you could love. That you had a soul. And a heart."

"People see what they want to see," he said again. "Maybe if I had had a loyal wife, someone who fought as hard for me as you seem to fight for Marcus and his family, maybe I would have been a better man."

"Just leave." She refused to let his barbs hurt her anymore.

He looked up at her then took a step toward the gates. Haraka's men stood near either side of him, ready to grab him if he lurched back up the stairs to attack her.

"The disease is unpredictable," he said after a moment, glancing around the courtyard as if he was already taking inventory. "People die in their sleep without warning. Everyone knows that. You will never be able to close your eyes again without wondering if it is your turn to die. In the night, you will always wonder where I am."

She was unmoved by his threat. He would not get a reaction from her.

"If Marcus dies," he added, "I will hear about it. I will hear about it, and I will take action. Tullia is a lovely girl. She is young, and the young can often survive these diseases. I will be in need of a wife by then. She just might do."

"Get out!" Shoshan shouted, immediately angry with herself for her outburst. He had wanted to provoke her, and he had won.

Antonius's self-satisfied laugh made her grit her teeth as he sauntered toward the gate.

Shoshan returned at once to check on Tullia and pushed the window covering back to air out the room. She did not want the faintest trace of Antonius to linger. Besides, the fighting must have frightened Tullia. Sitting beside her, Shoshan murmured, assuring her that the danger was gone, that she could rest now.

A tear rolled down Tullia's cheek. Deep within Shoshan's mind, the sight of that tear registered like a bell ringing. Tullia was crying. Why was that so important?

A second later Shoshan nearly shouted with relief. Tullia had been too badly dehydrated to cry ever since Shoshan had arrived. Tears were a sign that life was returning to her body.

"Praise God," Shoshan breathed, smiling through her own tears now. "Praise God for every tear that flows."

Downstairs, Shoshan heard the gate clanging closed. Antonius had gone, but now a woman's unfamiliar voice rang out.

"I demand to see Tullia, right now!"

Shoshan peered out from the bedroom window.

An unfamiliar older woman, beautifully dressed in a blue robe, stood at the gate. Shoshan noticed the woman gripping the arm of the servant girl she had spoken to, looking for news of Jesus. Antonius had stopped beside the gate, watching the pair with interest.

"Where is Tullia?" the woman called, looking past Shoshan and into the courtyard. The woman's eyes darted back and forth across the courtyard.

The servant girl locked eyes with Shoshan, and Shoshan felt her heart speed up, as if preparing her to run. There was nowhere to run to. She was trapped, and this time, she had been caught in her own deception. It was a terrifying feeling.

The girl frowned, confused. "She is right there," she said, pointing to Shoshan.

"That is not Tullia," the woman snapped at the girl.

She addressed Shoshan directly next.

"My servant spoke to Tullia, and I am afraid she said things she should not have said. She can be so unflattering in her assessment of me, and of my intentions. I think she owes Tullia and me an apology."

The woman pushed the servant girl forward and looked expectantly at Shoshan.

"Well?" the woman said. "Go and fetch Tullia."

The woman looked at Antonius coldly, making a note of his worn and dirty robes. "Are you leaving or staying? Make up your mind. You cannot just stand there with the gate open. Not with a house like this."

"But this woman…" the girl said.

"Are you really so silly?" the woman turned to her, outraged. "This is not Tullia. It is clearly her…" She seemed to fumble for the words, then looked at the robes Shoshan was wearing more closely. An instant later, her eyes widened in recognition.

The woman took a step back, pushing the servant girl slightly in front, like a shield, as her face registered alarm. "Who are you? Where is Tullia?"

Shoshan opened her mouth to reply, but there was no easy answer.

"What have you done with the servants? Who are those men?" The neighbor eyed the hired men patrolling the courtyard. She looked next at Antonius, who stood in the path of the open gates, and her eyes narrowed.

"You are not one of them," she said, her eyes flicking back up to the lovely home rising over the courtyard.

Antonius smiled thinly, as if she had complimented him. Maybe he thought she had.

"I tried to tell you something was off," the girl said to her. "But you thought I was looking for an excuse to stir up rumors."

Antonius reached out to rest a hand on the woman's arm. "There is something you need to see upstairs."

"Guard!" the woman screamed, wresting her arm away from Antonius.

"Please, do not." Shoshan lurched forward, reaching for the woman.

It only alarmed her further, and she screamed louder this time. "Guard!"

"Tullia is pregnant and needs a midwife. Help us," Shoshan begged.

The heavy tread of boots echoed in the street. Clemens turned the corner, and behind him, the larger guard, the one who carried the cat-o'-nine-tails whip at his side. Terror flooded Shoshan's body. Shoving the woman out of the gates and knocking Antonius out of the way, Shoshan had only one thought. *Close the gates.*

Even a Roman guard could not enter the home of a government official without an invitation, surely.

"Tullia!" the neighbor yelled, looking upstairs before refocusing on Shoshan, fighting off her attempts to shove her away. "Where is Marcus? Why did he not send for the midwife?"

"I tried," Shoshan replied, watching the guards close the distance to the home. "Please, go and find one."

Shoshan succeeded in pushing the women away and grabbed the gates to swing them closed.

She was too late. Clemens, his chest rising and falling under his chest plate, stood in the gap. He towered over her. She could smell sweat and the grease he used to polish his armor. And something else, something unmistakable… What was it? She knew the smell but couldn't name it. Her fright made thought impossible.

Antonius grabbed the servant girl and faced the guard with the whip. "I have a witness this time."

This time? Had he gone to the guards already, and they rebuffed him? Antonius jerked the girl's arm, and she yelped. "Tell them. Tell them who this woman is."

The girl looked at Shoshan helplessly.

Shoshan looked away.

"She is Tullia, the mistress of this estate," the girl replied with a tremor in her voice. "At least, that is who she told me she was."

"I did not say that!" Shoshan pleaded with the guard who held the whip, even as he reached for her.

"That is not Tullia!" the neighbor declared. "I do not know who she is, or what she is doing here, but she is not Tullia."

"You and I know, do we not?" Antonius addressed Clemens.

Clemens angled his body away from Shoshan and whispered something to the other guard, who Shoshan guessed was his superior.

"This woman pretending to be Tullia? She is my wife, the one that everyone has seen me mourning for. Her real name is Shoshan, and she faked her own death three weeks ago. She was giving birth to our first child, and the child died. Shoshan lost her mind. She has been wandering the streets, claiming that Jesus resurrected her. She has caused no end of heartache for me. Not to mention the trouble she has caused the guards."

Antonius waited expectantly for the guards to arrest her.

The woman and her servant stared at Shoshan, a look of shock on each face.

Marcus made his way down the stairs, stopping midway to catch his breath. The commanding officer walked to the stairs, ready to assist a member of the elite class.

"Sir?" Clemens asked Marcus. "How much of what this man says is true?"

She sensed Marcus trying to summon his strength, and it was like he was straining to see a dim light in the distance. It was there, barely, but it was there. He only had to move toward it, and it would flare to life.

"Almost every word," Marcus admitted. "But there is one error. My sister did not fake her death. Did she, Antonius?"

Antonius laughed uneasily, looking at the guards to check their reaction before he spoke to Marcus again. "I paid for her grave, Marcus."

Marcus produced a thin sheet of parchment from his robe, handing it to the commander, the guard with the whip, who nodded at Clemens. He rushed forward to take it.

"It is a letter from the midwife who delivered Shoshan's baby," Marcus said. "The midwife will confirm that Shoshan and the baby died. The midwife also adds a detail about Antonius's involvement that you might find interesting."

Shoshan's whole body stopped as she stared at the letter in her brother's hand.

"Where did you get this?" she whispered, not taking her eyes off the letter.

"I received it the same day you died," he replied, and his voice seemed to grow steadier. "I always had people who reported back to me about you. I think it was because of what happened when we were children, when I left you alone… I could not have you in my life, not if I was going to transform myself into a respected Roman official. But I vowed long ago I would never take my eyes off you again."

Shoshan's legs buckled, and she grabbed the gate to hold herself up. She had never been alone, not in the way she thought. Her brother had always been there, even when he lost his way.

Antonius, in a flash of movement, grabbed the letter from Clemens and crumpled it. Then he ran through the gates and thrust it into a torch. Flames licked his hand, but he kept holding the letter up until it was engulfed in flames.

By the time Clemens grabbed him, only a second later, pulling him to the ground, the letter was a black, crumbling ball. Little embers of bright red papyrus floated down from Antonius's clenched hand, now black with soot. Enormous blisters puffed the skin she could see. The smell was terrible. Only when the letter was destroyed did he howl in pain, a piercing sound, and Clemens flinched.

Antonius grabbed the dagger on Clemens's belt. Clemens yelled and fought for control, but Antonius pushed him aside with astonishing strength, rushing straight at Shoshan, the blade aimed at her stomach.

Clemens threw himself in front of her, hands extended to stop the dagger, and the two men dropped to the ground.

Suddenly both men ceased their struggle, and Clemens was covered with a burst of blood across his abdomen. He looked down, wide-eyed in horror, pressing his palms into his stomach, then lifting them to his face, studying his hands. Shoshan rushed to his side, checking for the wound, the tear in the tunic.

"It is not mine," Clemens breathed. "The blood is not mine."

Standing and whirling to face Antonius, Shoshan saw a blood-stain on his abdomen growing wider and wider. He, not Clemens, had been stabbed, and now he was dying.

She moved to help him, but Clemens held out a stiff arm to stop her.

Meeting Clemens's gaze, she gently pushed his arm down. Kneeling beside Antonius, her throat closed with a knot of pain. He was dying. She didn't love him anymore, but she had once. Love made it impossible to let him go easily. He was a part of her, even if she didn't want him to be. He was a part of her first life, the life before this one.

"I am not sorry," he managed to say between unsteady breaths. "I will not apologize."

Clemens hovered over them both, listening.

Lifting her eyes, Shoshan looked past Clemens, and past even Marcus and the officer on the stairs. She looked for Haraka and saw him standing in the center of the courtyard, watching her. She willed him to see it, every moment of it. *This is what revenge does to a man.*

Finally, Haraka turned away, his head low.

"I just wanted something better," Antonius whispered, his eyes glazing over.

His words stung. *Better than what? Me? Our home, our future? Our daughter?*

"It is not too late," she said shaking him, trying to rouse him, to hold him on this side of eternity just a moment longer. "There is still time. Ask God to forgive you. Jesus has forgiven the men who crucified Him. He did not return for revenge but for redemption. You can still be redeemed."

Antonius's head rolled to the left, limp and heavy. He was gone. Where he had gone, she would not discover, she knew, not until she left this life again. No one moved or spoke for a second. There was a heaviness that had to be cleared away, a dullness that seemed to hang over the sun itself. Marcus collapsed, his knees giving way.

"Leave him," the commander barked at Clemens. Then he turned toward Marcus. "Get this man upstairs."

Clemens immediately stepped away from Shoshan and Antonius and lifted Marcus from the ground. Shoshan watched him carry her brother upstairs, knowing he would find Tullia and discover the plague.

The commanding officer, who had seen and heard everything from the stairs, fled the home immediately, his face dark with an emotion she could not identify.

Shoshan stood and held out her hands in supplication as he passed her. A quarantine now would be fatal.

"Tullia's water has broken," Clemens called. "Go and get a midwife."

She ran.

CHAPTER TWENTY-FIVE

Dusk approached. As night fell, Sabbath ended and people emerged from their homes. Vendors served spiced wine and roasted chickpeas again, and slowly, the city came to life.

Upstairs, Tullia labored.

Shoshan and Haraka waited in the courtyard. Tullia had needed fresh air, and the room was small, so everyone other than Marcus and the midwife had been forced to leave. The midwife raised an eyebrow at Marcus's insistence on staying, but Shoshan knew he was too afraid of losing Tullia to leave her.

The raven landed in the courtyard, cawing. The sound was harsh, and Shoshan swept it away with a flick of her arm. Haraka, sitting with her, watched but did not stop her. The hired men sat on benches in the courtyard, elbows resting on their knees, waiting.

Shoshan had quickly reached the midwife and brought her back to the house. Now Tullia had the help she needed, and a midwife had medicines, including poppy juice. Pain and fever were common in laboring mothers. The midwife would be ready. If she had noticed that Tullia was ill, she had said nothing. Maybe a midwife cared less about the laws of Rome and more about the life of the baby and mother.

But as Tullia labored, Shoshan was uneasy. Even now, it mattered whether the baby was a boy or a girl. Only a boy would secure the estate for Marcus. It was a cruel arithmetic that gave boys such value. Shoshan wanted her girl more than anything in the world. She would have been happy to live the rest of her life with her daughter. But now, all that mattered was that Tullia either delivered a boy who survived or lived to try again. If the baby was a girl, the estate would still be at risk if Marcus died.

The scraping of the gate caught everyone's attention. When she lifted her eyes, Clemens stood in the courtyard.

Standing, she motioned for him to join her nearer the pool, where they could have more privacy.

"Have you come to arrest me?" she asked.

He shook his head and seemed unable to speak. After licking his lips and pausing as if to collect his thoughts, he tried again.

"I came to warn you."

"About what?"

Antonius was dead. Although the letter had been destroyed, she had witnesses now that Antonius had tried to cover up the truth.

"You need to leave Jerusalem, as soon as you can." Clemens met her gaze, but this time, his eyes were clear. His face seemed different too, relaxed maybe. The lines of anger that compressed together on his forehead were smoother.

"I do not understand." She didn't, not any of this.

"My commanding officer—do you remember what you said when Antonius was dying?"

"Not clearly," Shoshan replied as a connection began to form. She remembered the bloody cat-o'-nine-tails at the commander's side. No other guard she had seen carried one. Could he have been the guard who scourged Jesus?

"He has been recalled to Rome," Clemens continued. "He had a breakdown of sorts."

"I do not understand what that has to do with me. Why do I have to leave Jerusalem?"

"Because Caesar spends a lot of money to train and equip us. My commander was the pride of his forces. But every word you said tore him apart. The shock of realizing what we did to the Son of God has ruined one of Rome's most feared military men."

Shoshan remembered then how she spoke of Jesus forgiving everyone, even the men who crucified Him. The commander knew what he had done to Jesus, and now knew who Jesus was.

Clemens said, "Forgiveness is the only weapon I have ever seen that could bring my commander to his knees. He is not the same man since he heard you say that. He wants nothing more to do with swords and whips. He only wants to know more of Jesus. Caesar is irate."

Shoshan paused, thinking it all through.

"What about you?" she finally asked. "You look different. Lighter, somehow."

"I still had a job to do after my commander left. I had to find anyone who claimed to be resurrected, including anyone claiming to be the resurrected Jesus, and arrest them. But…"

The realization struck Shoshan with great force.

"You met Him?" she whispered. He was still in Jerusalem. It had not been a whole month since His death, but He must still be in the area.

Clemens smiled, looking almost bashful, then gave a quick nod. "I do not think I would have believed anything He said, if not for you. I would have thought He was a conman, really."

"I never told you about Jesus," she replied.

"You did," he insisted. "I learned about Him when you kneeled in the dirt to forgive your husband. He had tried to kill you. Maybe he even succeeded the first time, I do not know. I am still working through that story. But he almost killed your brother, and he destroyed an important letter that could have proved your story. When I looked down, you had his blood on your face and dirt from the street on your robes. But all you wanted was for him to find forgiveness."

Clemens took a long breath, then sighed it out. "Who does that?" he added weakly.

"Jesus does," she replied. Clemens looked at her then, and in his eyes she saw recognition. Jesus had done that for him too, offering forgiveness in the mess of his choices.

"I have a daughter," Marcus declared in the dark hours just before dawn the following morning, standing at the top of the stairs, holding a newborn. "She is strong, like her mother."

The midwife stepped around him and made her way to the kitchen, where Haraka was preparing the day's bread.

"Tullia?" Shoshan asked, moving to stand at the bottom of the stairs.

"Come and see her," Marcus replied. Shoshan took the steps two at a time, pausing only to glance at the baby before entering the bedroom and finding Tullia sitting up. Her eyes were closed, but her cheeks had a tinge of pink. That was a good sign. It was not the red of a fever.

Shoshan crossed the room and sat beside Tullia and took her hand. Tullia's eyes opened, just a little, and she smiled.

"She is beautiful," Shoshan whispered. "What will you name her?"

"I do not know," Tullia replied. "What did you name your daughter?"

Shoshan stopped. "I did not."

Tullia's eyes opened again. "Why not?"

That same knot of grief constricted Shoshan's throat again. "She died before I could." She did not repeat the other part of her story, that she had died as well. Tullia did not need to hear that right now.

"We will name them together, then," Tullia said.

Tullia named her daughter Eliana, meaning, "my God has answered," and Shoshan chose the name Aviva, meaning, "springtime," for her daughter. She had given birth in the spring, and she knew that someday, the spring would come again. She and Aviva would be together forever.

Shoshan finished packing her little bag. A change of clothes, money for travel, a parchment written with the names of plants she would need. Marcus had encouraged her to buy expensive parchment instead of simple papyrus for the list. She'd never held such solid, sturdy paper. It would last through many journeys, and she was grateful.

"You are really leaving?" Haraka asked. He stood in the kitchen doorway, watching her descend the stairs.

This was a conversation they had already had, a dozen times or more.

"Yes, and you will stay," she replied. "This is your home now, Haraka."

"Home is my mother," he replied. "But I will live here until she and I are reunited."

She embraced him and smiled as his arms encircled her waist. He held on tightly, and she felt his shoulders shake. She kissed the top of his head and held him until he let go.

"I will return whenever I can," she said. "There are many people who suffer with this illness. They need help."

"You are not scared you could catch it too?" he asked. "You could die."

"I have already died once, sweet friend. I am not afraid of that."

"But if you die, we would be parted," he insisted.

"Not forever," Shoshan reminded him. Over the last few months, Haraka had slowly come to faith in Jesus. He was willing to trust the One who cared for the birds, the One who had given life to Shoshan. He wanted to walk with Jesus too.

The reminder of heaven encouraged him. He straightened his posture and nodded.

"Do you think you will ever see Him again?" he asked. He had so many questions. Marcus had hired a tutor for him, treating him like a son instead of a servant. Haraka was going to have a very good life. Marcus's household possessions had been stolen, but the bulk of his money was in a treasury in Rome. He would, in time, be able to restore his home.

"The disciples said He ascended," she replied. The disciples and followers of Jesus had told her amazing stories after she reconnected with them. They spoke of tongues of fire and Jesus ascending to heaven. She felt a pang of regret that she'd missed all that, but her work had been here. This is where Jesus had wanted her to be. She had to trust that whatever miracles she missed out on seeing, He would amply bless her in different ways instead.

For now, there was work to be done. The Roman plague isolated people when they most needed care and comfort. She had a good working knowledge now of how to care for the victims, and she had very little fear. Jesus had sent her here, to care for Marcus and Tullia, but He must have wanted her to go out into the world after this. She knew how much suffering there was.

She walked to the gate, then paused and looked back. Marcus and Tullia stood in the courtyard, their daughter in Tullia's arms. Haraka stood next to Marcus, holding his hand.

She released a deep breath, looking at them and up at this house. What a work of redemption Jesus had done, for all of them. The past was dead and gone. Each of them had new life and love, the love of Him, in their hearts.

She would see them all again, she knew, no matter what happened in this life. Until then, she would do His work and love as He loved, waiting for the day when she heard His voice calling her name once more.

FROM THE AUTHOR

Dear Reader,

The detail of the resurrected saints is only included in the Gospel of Matthew. It is a curious detail that challenges our imagination. I wondered who the resurrected ones were, why Matthew did not give us more details, and what became of them after Jesus's ascension. We can assume they went on living in their physical bodies, but they must have had many questions. Can you imagine being resurrected hundreds of years after your death and living in the world, waiting for Jesus to return? They also faced the reality of dying for a second time.

It must not have been easy for them, just as our conversion isn't always easy for us. When we are reborn, we are changed, but our circumstances are not always improved. That's the real mystery to many of us. The all-powerful God lives within us, and we walk through a difficult life, facing hardships with the love of Christ in our hearts. Love transforms us, even in the midst of pain.

I believe that love transforms the world too, as we spread the fragrance of Christ wherever we go. Maybe that's one reason our circumstances are often still difficult after we accept Christ. He is relying on us to spread His love in those very circumstances.

That's an honor and a comfort.

I pray you feel that comfort today, no matter what you face. Christ within you is the message of hope and love that this world needs.

Blessings to you,
Ginger Garrett

KEEPING THE FAITH

1. Why do you think some people were raised back to life when Jesus was resurrected? Why does the gospel writer Matthew not include any more details, such as names?
2. Shoshan is surprised that her resurrection-life is not easy. Her body was raised, but her circumstances were still difficult. How does that reflect the reality of receiving Jesus as your Savior, yet facing challenging hardships?
3. If you heard of the dead raised back to life in your city, how would you react? Who would you turn to for more information and confirmation?
4. How would your life be different if you hadn't become a Christian?
5. What questions of faith did Shoshan struggle with? Have you struggled with these same questions?

MARSHES, MOSQUITOES, AND MEDICINES: BATTLING MALARIA IN THE ANCIENT WORLD

By Reverend Jane Willan, MS, MDiv

Malaria was a silent yet potent force in ancient Rome and Jerusalem, shaping lives, cultures, and beliefs. Its presence influenced medical practices, societal norms, and religious interpretations, marking it as a significant yet often overlooked factor in the fabric of these civilizations. The struggle against this invisible enemy reveals much about the resilience of the communities of Rome and Jerusalem, their approaches to health and disease, and how they sought to understand and control the natural world around them.

Malaria, a disease transmitted by the Anopheles mosquito, thrived in the warm, humid climate of the Mediterranean basin, making ancient Rome, Jerusalem, and the rural regions of Judea ripe environments for its spread. In Rome, the combination of bustling urban life with stagnant water sources, such as the city's marshes, created ideal breeding grounds for mosquitoes. The city's aqueducts and the Tiber River also facilitated the spread of malaria by providing mosquitoes with habitats close to human dwellings.

In Jerusalem and surrounding Judea, the situation was somewhat different but equally conducive to the spread of malaria. The agricultural practices and the reliance on water collection methods, including cisterns and storage pits, created pockets of still water where mosquitoes could breed. Rural communities living near these water sources were particularly vulnerable. The environmental conditions and the limited understanding of disease transmission meant that malaria could spread with little to stop it.

The impact of malaria on these regions was profound. In Rome, it affected both the rich and poor, leading to high mortality rates and significant social and economic disruption. In Jerusalem and Judea, the effects of malaria would have been felt in the daily lives of peasants and farmers, stonemasons, and shopkeepers, impacting agricultural productivity, business, and community health.

In the ancient world, the battle against malaria was fought with a mix of emerging medical knowledge and traditional remedies deeply rooted in spiritual beliefs. In Rome, physicians drew upon the humoral theory of medicine that attributed the disease to imbalances among bodily fluids. They believed that malaria was caused by these imbalances, often attributing its symptoms to bad air or "miasma." Treatment focused on rebalancing the humors using methods such as diet regulation and administering herbal remedies. While the physicians of Rome lacked a precise understanding of the disease's transmission, their observational skills and systematic approach to treatment laid the groundwork for future medical advances.

Understanding and treating malaria in Jerusalem was very different. The Jewish people, deeply connected to their spiritual traditions, would have sought cures and protections in prayers, rituals, and the wisdom of the Torah. Alongside these spiritual practices, they employed a variety of herbal remedies derived from local plants and minerals. These might have included the use of willow bark, which contains a precursor to aspirin called salicin, to reduce fever, a common symptom of malaria.

In Rome, the constant presence of malaria had significant repercussions on everyday life and the broader societal structure. For instance, efforts were made to drain swamps and marshes around urban areas, notably the Pontine Marshes, though with limited success due to the engineering capabilities of the time. Public baths, a staple of Roman civilization, also played a role in public health, promoting hygiene to combat malaria and other diseases that thrived in urban settings.

The impact of malaria extended to the military, influencing the strategic planning of campaigns. Roman legions avoided marshy areas known to be breeding grounds for mosquitoes. Military encampments were located in higher, drier areas to protect troops from disease. Despite these precautions, malaria often decimated legions, affecting the outcomes of military campaigns and, by extension, the expansion and defense of the Roman Empire.

In Jerusalem and the broader region of Judea, malaria similarly infiltrated the social and spiritual realms. The disease's prevalence influenced religious practices, as prayers and rituals sought divine intervention for healing and protection against illnesses. Pilgrimages, central to Jewish religious life, were not exempt from the threat of malaria. Pilgrims traveling through or to malaria-endemic areas were at risk, potentially limiting the number of individuals able to undertake these spiritual journeys.

The social fabric of Jewish communities was also affected. The communal nature of Jewish life meant that the spread of diseases like malaria could have devastating effects on families and communities. This necessitated a communal response to care for the sick and a reliance on shared knowledge of herbal remedies and traditional healing practices.

In ancient times, illness and disease were often viewed through a spiritual lens. People's understanding of diseases like malaria was deeply intertwined with the spiritual and the divine, reflecting the broader worldview that saw the hand of gods or God in the workings of the natural world.

In Roman society, the pantheon of gods was believed to directly influence the health and well-being of individuals and the community. Illnesses like malaria were seen as manifestations of divine displeasure or punishment for societal or personal failings. Romans believed appeasing the gods was essential to restoring health and preventing disease. This belief led to specific rituals and sacrifices. For instance, the Romans might make offerings to Febris, the goddess associated explicitly with fever, to gain relief from malaria. These practices were part of a broader system of religious observances that sought to maintain harmony between the human and divine realms, with health seen as a reflection of this balance.

Similarly, in Jerusalem and the broader Jewish community, illness was often understood within a framework of divine testing or punishment. The Hebrew Scriptures contain numerous references to sickness and health, framing them as part of God's covenant with His people. Diseases like malaria could be interpreted as tests of faith or as punishments for disobedience to God's laws.

However, the Jewish response to such illnesses differed from the Roman approach. Instead of sacrifices to appease a pantheon of gods, the Jewish people devoted themselves to prayer, repentance, and adherence to religious laws. Healing was sought through invoking God's mercy, emphasizing communal prayer and the belief in God's power to heal. The prophets often called for a return to righteousness to restore health to the individual and the community.

References to diseases that resemble malaria can also be found in biblical texts, providing indirect evidence of the disease's impact. Leviticus 26:16 says "Then I will do this to you: I will bring on you sudden terror, wasting diseases and fever that will destroy your sight and sap your strength." The "wasting diseases and fever" mentioned here could be interpreted as symptoms indicative of various diseases, including malaria, given the historical prevalence of the disease in regions close to the ancient Near East. The mention of fever that destroys the sight and saps the strength suggests a severe illness that affects the body profoundly, akin to how malaria can cause high fevers, shaking chills, and other intense symptoms.

The ancient world's confrontation with malaria, fraught with challenges and marked by resilience, offers enduring lessons for us today. Modern societies can navigate the complexities of health crises by valuing proactive public health measures, fostering community resilience, integrating holistic approaches to healing, and balancing innovation with historical wisdom. The ancient struggle against malaria is not just a historical curiosity but a lesson in faith, inspiration, and instruction for facing the challenges of the future.

Fiction Author

GINGER GARRETT

Ginger Garrett is the author of multiple titles from Guideposts, all available at shopguideposts.org. In addition to numerous novels and nonfiction titles, she has ghostwritten popular books in both the children's and adult markets.

A popular speaker and frequent media guest, she's been featured by media across the country including Fox News, *USA Today*, *Library Journal*, 104.7 The Fish Atlanta, and more. Ginger lives in Atlanta with her family and rescues wayward giant-breed dogs.

Nonfiction Author

REVEREND JANE WILLAN, MS, MDiv

Reverend Jane Willan writes contemporary women's fiction, mystery novels, church newsletters, and a weekly sermon.

Jane loves to set her novels amid church life. She believes that ecclesiology, liturgy, and church lady drama make for twisty plots and quirky characters. When not working at the church or creating new adventures for her characters, Jane relaxes at her favorite local bookstore, enjoying coffee and a variety of carbohydrates with frosting. Otherwise, you might catch her binge-watching a streaming series or hiking through the Connecticut woods with her husband and rescue dog, Ollie.

Jane earned a Bachelor of Arts degree from Hiram College, majoring in Religion and History, a Master of Science degree from Boston University, and a Master of Divinity from Vanderbilt University.

*Read on for a sneak peek of another exciting story
in the Mysteries & Wonders of the Bible series!*

GARDEN OF SECRETS:
Adah's Story
by Texie Susan Gregory

*Noah, a man of the soil, proceeded to plant a vineyard. When he
drank some of its wine, he became drunk and lay uncovered inside
his tent. Ham, the father of Canaan, saw his father naked and told
his two brothers outside. But Shem and Japheth took a garment and
laid it across their shoulders; then they walked in backward and
covered their father's naked body. Their faces were turned the other
way so that they would not see their father naked.*
~Genesis 9:20–23 (NIV)~

Noah crouched by the spitting fire. He shielded his grizzled face as he
relived the shame that burned hotter than the flames. That long-
ago memory yet ached—the near loss of his sons' respect from his lapse
of judgment, his self-indulgence. Blessed be Elohim, the Creator, who'd
used that reckless indulgence to reveal the worthiest of his three sons.

He prodded the burning logs apart with a stick, its edge shining
silver, gilded in the flame's light. Bold stars spun into the dark,

hissing, singeing the leather of his tunic before their lives snuffed out—as his would soon be.

The heat dissipated, the chill edged closer. No matter. What would happen next demanded concealment, the covert mystery of night.

In the dimming light, he glanced at Japheth, sprawled on his back, snoring softly. A good man, this beloved son. He'd assisted Shem in covering his—Noah's—nakedness. He would do well in life even as the seduction of uncertainty lured him to venture ever farther into unknown lands. Thank the Almighty, Japheth's cherished wife would temper his bold impulses, keep him worshiping the Creator.

He shifted to study Ham, listening to his son's heavy, steady breath, although Ham—master of deception— could hold himself so still one was never sure if he was sleeping. Ham moved with uncanny stealth, and it often seemed he appeared from nowhere. It had been Ham who'd found him drunk and run to tell his brothers. Poor Ham, forever seeking approval and acceptance, with neither the wisdom nor the kindness of his brothers.

Noah grimaced as he stood, his knees crackling in protest, his back slow to straighten. He hobbled to where Shem lay. This son— he'd been told—had hurried to cover his father's shame, even averting his eyes as had Japheth. Shem, more than the other two, sought the wisdom of the Almighty.

He nudged Shem with the ball of his foot. Shem bolted to his feet, drawing his weapons in one practiced motion. In the dimming firelight, Noah held a finger to his lips and motioned him to follow.

A distance from the others, Noah withdrew his dagger. He fumbled with the knot as he loosened the sheath from his belt. Drawing a thin line with the flint blade so only the top layer of the sheath parted, he slit it lengthwise. Fingers trembling, he extracted a scrap of rolled, flattened leather.

In the starless night, he knew Shem would not see the tears stinging his eyes nor that he held the scrap to his heart. Noah caressed the worn leather surface before raising it to his lips.

"Lord, will You not relent, allow us to return to the Garden, to Your paradise?"

There was no answer. There had never been an answer, no matter how fervently he'd pleaded through the years.

"Shem, my son, I entrust you with the world's most precious possession." He paused, willed his voice to remain steady. "This map marks the place of beginning."

He sensed Shem startle and knew his son's quick mind understood.

"The Garden, *Abba*?"

Noah nodded then remembered that such a small motion might not be visible. "Yes. Etched by a daughter of Eve on a clay tablet."

"Abba, so long ago. How…?"

"Someone drew it on leather. Through the years it has been recopied whenever the leather begins to brittle. The previous map is always destroyed. Others may claim possession of the map, but only ours shows the flaming swords, the true entrance."

Cradling the reminder of wholeness—the joy of walking with the Creator—Noah kissed it, once more inhaling its earthy scent. He fumbled for Shem's hand and curled his son's fingers around the treasure but did not release it. To do so acknowledged his end was nearing. Soon he would walk with his fathers.

"Yours is the eleventh generation from Adam. Someday, perhaps the Lord will order the flaming swords sheathed, reveal a way to return to paradise, allow us into His holy presence."

Embracing the sacred moment, Noah placed his hand on his son's shoulder, aware of their connection beyond familial ties, beyond memories of survival. For now, they stood not as parent and child but as two men bonded in ancient ritual.

With a deep sigh, Noah released the map. The responsibility, the entrusted duty, was no longer his. Shem must bear the burden of knowledge.

They returned to the camp without speaking. As Noah lowered himself to his bedroll, he scanned the fireside. Japheth had turned on his side, no longer snoring.

Ham was nowhere to be seen.

Many Generations Later, 435 BC
A small village east of Beit She'an

Adah measured out her words with flat truth—facts—no emotion, no inflection. "I have been sold—indentured. I am a slave."

If Jonah cringed or shifted away, she'd know and accept his truth. She searched her beloved's face for the slightest sign of revulsion or rejection. They'd never marry, but would her slavery repulse him?

His family abhorred the sale of relatives into slavery, and she was the third of her abba's daughters to be sold. No one, least of all she, would judge Jonah for walking away. In truth, he had no choice. She was unacceptable to his family.

Disregarding proper behavior, Jonah reached for her hand and brought it to his lips, the tenderness testing her will to remain dry-eyed and distant. She'd not bind him with tears or pleas.

"Adah, never doubt I will come for you. I am a hard worker, a fast worker." He flexed the bulges on his arms.

Adah blushed and wished she could run her fingers along those smooth muscles.

"As soon as I have earned enough to redeem you from servitude, I will claim you as my wife."

"Claim a slave as your wife?" She pulled away, voice rising as she dropped the pretense of indifference. "Abba sold me to them for six years."

"It will not be that long, I promise you."

"In six years, they can marry me to their son. Abba will never buy me back…" Her voice broke.

They stood in silence as the breeze freshened, ruffling the tall grasses and dappling them with shadows of acacia leaves. Nearby, birds called, dancing among the tree branches, flitting near, then darting away.

A rogue curl escaped from behind Jonah's ear. Adah imagined standing close enough to wrap it around her finger before securing it in place—a wife's privilege. She studied him, memorizing the slope of his neck, the curls of his beard, and the way emotions chased each other across his face, darkening his eyes, crinkling his forehead, pursing his lips.

His frown flickered before a smile softened his face. "They cannot marry you to their son if we are already betrothed."

Her dear man was a dreamer. "Jonah, you know your abba will never agree—"

"But, Adah, *we* have agreed."

We? Her nervous laughter did not seem to faze him. He held out both hands, smiling when she immediately placed hers within his open palms. "Adah, before the Almighty gave the law to Moses at Sinai, two people could choose to be together without a contract negotiated by their parents. Adah, step back in time with me. I choose you to be my wife."

An endearing uncertainty softened Jonah's usual brash confidence to stuttering. "W-will you choose me?"

"Jonah ben David, of course, I choose you, but—"

"Stop, Adah. We have chosen, we have promised. Leave it there. We will take the next step of our betrothal as soon as possible. For now, it is our secret. Trust me. I will redeem you. We will face our parents. If they oppose us, my uncle, Aaron ben Hassenaah, in Jerusalem, might help us." He grinned, his wide smile cocky once again. "I have always been his favorite nephew. For now, we have done all we can do. Leave it there."

Adah loved the confidence and innocence in his eyes. If it came to be, she'd give thanks all her days. She swallowed past the lump in her throat.

All that was good and kind seemed to reside in Jonah. It was as if the Lord God had filled Jonah to the brim of his being with joy and gentleness. Adah blinked away a tear. This amazing man loved *her.* His parents might not approve of her family, but she would work hard to win their favor.

If she and Jonah did marry, she could claim his sisters as her own. This time, the tear fell. Years ago, when she was a small child, Abba had sold her two sisters. She still remembered the anguish of her *imma*'s face and—though her sisters' features had blurred—she had never forgotten their wails as they were led away. It was not something she liked to think about.

Jonah tugged at her hand. "You seem sad."

"I was remembering my sisters and wondering if they are still alive."

"If they are, we will find them, and I will build an enormous house, and they can live with us. Your little brother too. We will live in a town large enough for a synagogue and praise the Almighty every day. We will go to Jerusalem for the holy days."

Adah laughed, seizing the joy of hope and dreams. "I will light the Shabbat candles, and we will always have guests."

"You must become an excellent cook while you are away."

His words sobered her. "Six years seems forever."

"Adah, I will come before then. There is no risk of you becoming betrothed to their son. It is impossible. Trust me." The lines around his eyes tightened. "I will make certain you are never under your abba's roof again. You have been nothing more than a slave to him, and I struggle to treat him with any respect, knowing he hires you out to do the lowest work in other houses."

Adah lowered her eyes in shame. Everyone knew her abba's disgraceful ways—his laziness, his cunning, his constant debt.

"Jonah, when we are married…" She blushed. "Can we move far away?"

A shadow darkened his face. "Do you mean to live among foreigners? Strangers?"

"Maybe not foreigners but among our people who do not know my abba? And are they truly strangers if we all worship Adonai, the one true God?"

"Adah, this is what we must do. We must pray for Adonai to guide us to a place where we can learn more about Him. We are His people, and I am certain He will answer us."

Adah nodded but did not speak. Although she knew Adonai was the one true God, she was not sure He knew or cared about her. Maybe He would guide Jonah, and she could follow Jonah's direction.